GRANDPA'S STORIES

Grandpa's Stories

Joe Kretoski, Jr.

ELM HILL

A Division of
HarperCollins Christian Publishing

www.elmhillbooks.com

Grandpa's Stories

Published in Nashville, Tennessee, by Elm Hill, an imprint of Thomas Nelson. Elm Hill and Thomas Nelson are registered trademarks of HarperCollins Christian

Elm Hill titles may be purchased in bulk for educational, business, fund-raising, or sales promotional use. For information, please e-mail SpecialMarkets@ThomasNelson.com.

Scripture quotations marked AMP are from the Amplified˚ Bible. Copyright © 1954, 1958, 1962, 1964, 1965, 1987 by The Lockman Foundation. Used by permission. (www.Lockman.org)

Scripture quotations marked ESV are from the ESV˚ Bible (The Holy Bible, English Standard Version˚). Copyright © 2001 by Crossway, a publishing ministry of Good News Publishers. Used by permission. All rights reserved.

Scripture quotations marked KJV are from the King James Version. Public domain.

Scripture quotations marked NASB are from New American Standard Bible˚. Copyright © 1960, 1962, 1963, 1968, 1971, 1972, 1973, 1975, 1977, 1995 by The Lockman Foundation. Used by permission. (www.Lockman.org)

Scripture quotations marked NIV are from the Holy Bible, New International Version˚, NIV˚. Copyright © 1973, 1978, 1984, 2011 by Biblica, Inc.˚ Used by permission of Zondervan. All rights reserved worldwide. www.Zondervan.com. The "NIV" and "New International Version" are trademarks registered in the United States Patent and Trademark Office by Biblica, Inc.˚

Scripture quotations marked NKJV are from the New King James Version˚. © 1982 by Thomas Nelson. Used by permission. All rights reserved.

Scripture quotations marked NLT are from the Holy Bible, New Living Translation. © 1996, 2004, 2007, 2013, 2015 by Tyndale House Foundation. Used by permission of Tyndale House Publishers, Inc., Carol Stream, Illinois 60188. All rights reserved.

Scripture quotations marked WEB are from the World English Bible˚. Public domain.

Library of Congress Cataloging-in-Publication Data

Library of Congress Control Number: 2018952691

ISBN 978-1-595558558 (Paperback)
ISBN 978-1-595558695 (Hardbound)
ISBN 978-1-595558770 (eBook)

INTRODUCTION

My mother was a very funny person who could mesmerize people with her stories. There were times when she entertained her family, and we would fill the house with laughter. It did not matter if we had heard that particular story twenty-five times, it was still hilarious to us and only got better with time. My mother went to Heaven in 2001 and may still be making people laugh with her humorous stories. The problem is that when she left her family for that wonderful place, I could only remember parts of her stories. Now when my three sisters and I get together, we can sometimes piece back together some of her stories, but because of the frailty of our minds, much has been forgotten. I do think my sisters remember much more than I do. Some of her stories have been lost entirely. That is rather unfortunate, but that is the main reason why I wrote *Grandpa's Stories*. When I am reunited with my mother, I don't want my family, especially my grandchildren, to forget my stories. Growing up, I had many unique experiences. Some were good, some were bad, and some were supernatural; while some were just life, they all molded me into the man I have become. I did not want these experiences and the life lessons instilled in me because of them to be lost to my family. I also wanted my grandchildren to be aware of their legacy. My parents were people of great faith who loved Jesus with every fiber of their beings. God radically saved and changed them. They desperately desired that their children, grandchildren, great-grandchildren, etc. would be "born again" and then have a lifelong relationship with God.

When I began writing *Grandpa's Stories*, my expectations were rather small. I planned to share a few stories, and it would be done, but the stories just kept coming, so I just kept writing. When I began to write I would relive the emotions of that story, and my memory would come alive. The memory portion just astounded me. I am an older guy who easily forgets things, but I was emotionally overwhelmed as these stories flooded my old brain. I experienced a myriad of emotions, which included crying, laughing, sadness, praise, thankfulness, etc. I would think that I was finally done with the book, and suddenly I would remember another story. I would wake up in the night and have stories flowing through my head. I would write down titles and just begin to write and then feel the story. Sometimes it was difficult to get to bed, because I had to finish a story, and at other times I could not wait to begin writing in the morning. Although this book is finished, I am not done writing. I am rather certain that there will be another book, probably titled *Grandpa's Dog Stories*. I already have close to forty titles written down that are beginning to cause the gears in my brain to engage.

This book could be used in many ways—as a daily devotional, reading for pleasure, to open up discussion for character building, for family devotions, or possibly a bedtime story. The list could continue, but I hope that you enjoy reading this book as much as I had writing it. May these stories inspire you as much as they have inspired me. If you are not one of my grandkids, just pretend that you are as you read these stories. May God bless you.

—Grandpa

CONTENTS

Sticks and Stones May Break My Bones, But Words Will Never Hurt Me

The saying "sticks and stones may break my bones, but words will never hurt me" has been around for a long time. I remember even as a young boy hearing this expression from neighborhood kids. The problem is that it is a big, fat lie. Words are extremely powerful and can have a very negative or positive affect. I am going to tell you a story of when there was great potential for negativity, but it turned out to be a very positive experience.

Your great-grandpa and I were going to go to the Shenandoah River to fish for smallmouth bass and channel catfish. The Shenandoah River is my all-time favorite river. It flows through parts of Virginia, Maryland, and West Virginia, and eventually flows into the Potomac River at Harper's Ferry, West Virginia. It is a large, wide, sometimes wild, and dangerous river—especially for a young kid fishing. I started fishing this river when I was around ten years old, and I don't mean just from the shore. I wet-waded this river from the beginning. I remember white-water rafters drifting by me out in the middle of this river. There were times when we did not discuss our fishing excursions with Great-Grandma Kretoski. She would have only worried about her baby boy.

On this particular day there had been rain that had the potential to make the rivers rise quickly. All the rain draining from the mountains and creeks can cause flooding in a hurry. My dad warned me not to take chances wading the river if it was too high. I told him I would try to be careful. Dad walked down the tracks several hundred yards to fish one of his favorite "holes." I entered the river and realized the river was higher than usual. I knew that I needed to cross rapids to get to one of my favorite "holes." I had waded out nearly to the middle of the river and was on the edge of the rapids. These rapids were approximately fifty feet wide and at least one hundred yards long. I stood on the edge of the rapids and debated with myself whether I should really try to cross them. I kept thinking about the good fishing that was on the other side of the rapids. My thinking kept changing from "You can do this" and then flip to "Joey, don't be stupid." So after a few minutes, what do you think I did? You are right! I tried to cross the rapids. I allowed the allure of big, small-mouth bass to cloud my better judgment. I took a risk that could have cost me my life. I began wading out into those rapids and did not realize how much the river had risen. I was out in the middle of the rapids and was stuck. I could not move my feet, because the force of the water was extremely strong. I had water hitting me so hard that it was cascading over my shoulders and was trying to pull me into the rocky rapids. The water was over waist-high deep, and I was in a bad predicament. I was struggling not to be swept into the rapids and happened to see my dad way downstream. I began hollering as loudly as I could and waving as much as I could. Finally he looked up and saw me, and waved back to me to indicate that he had seen me. He waded out of the river and began walking back up the tracks. I was hanging on for dear life. The water was pounding me, and I was stuck. Of course, I was thinking to myself that I was stupid and an idiot. Why didn't I just listen to my dad? Why didn't I just use common sense? It seemed like an eternity, but my dad eventually waded out and got to the edge of the rapids. He waded into the rapids carefully as far as he could and stuck out his fishing pole to me. He had broken his pole down into two pieces to make it stronger. I could barely reach it but finally gripped it with one hand and began to inch my way toward your great-grandpa. Slowly but surely, I crept toward Dad, and finally he stretched his hand out and pulled me to safety.

At this point most dads would have made very critical and negative comments to their sons, but my dad did not. He knew that his son did stupid things, was strong-willed, and did not always use the brain that God had given him. At this point he kind of shook his head, gave me a little smile, and said, "You're my boy." He did not criticize me but affirmed me as his son. This was one of the most powerful moments of my life. Is it any wonder that my father became my best friend and confidant?

Grandkids, there will be times in life when you will not always make the right decisions. Your thinking will become clouded like Grandpa's did. This is the time you need to call out to your Heavenly Father for help. He will rescue you. Don't be swept down the rapids of life. Also, be very careful when making decisions. Seek God's will, and listen to His voice.

One more thing to remember is that words are extremely powerful. Always try to be sensitive and kind to others. Choose your words carefully, especially when you are hurt or angry. You don't always have to say what you think. When you have your own kids, be strong, but always think of how influential your words are.

"A soft answer turns away wrath, but a harsh word stirs up anger."
PROVERBS 15:1 (NKJV)

ARE THERE REALLY
GUARDIAN ANGELS?

This story occurred when Grandpa was nine or ten years old. My father was a Free Methodist minister. There was a time he pastored at Nain, which was several miles from Fairmont and Rivesville, West Virginia. That particular conference of the Free Methodist Church had their yearly camp meeting at Black Hills, which is somewhere between Fairmont and Arthurdale. It was camp meeting time, and Grandpa was skipping church that evening. I was wandering around the campgrounds and decided to go to the bathroom. There was no running water, so Grandpa was walking down the path to the outside bathroom. If my memory serves me correctly, the male side was a six- or eight-holer and very stinky. I thought you might just want that little bit of information. The path to the bathroom was like an upside-down Y. Two paths connected into one main path. I began walking down the path that was on the right, and suddenly I literally felt a Power pick me up and move me several feet down the path. I was rather flabbergasted but happened to look back down the path. What do you think I saw? I saw a very large copperhead snake coiled on the pathway where I would have walked! I would have stepped right on the copperhead if that Power had not picked me up and moved me down the path. That was a supernatural act of God. I like to think that it was my own guardian angel. My mom and dad would daily pray for God's

5

protection over their children, and He definitely answered their prayers that evening as I skipped church.

"For He will command His angels concerning you to guard you in all your ways."

PSALM 91:11 (NIV)

SMOKE HOLE COPPERHEAD

Smoke Hole is found in eastern West Virginia in the Allegheny Mountains. The South Potomac River flows eighteen miles through this beautiful, pristine river gorge. There are several stories of how Smoke Hole received its name. One is that the Indians would smoke their meat in the caves located in the gorge. Another is that the fog rising off the river looks like smoke. Yet another would be that the early settlers were moonshiners and that you could see the smoke rising from the stills. I kind of like the "fog version." I have seen that fog rise off that river with my own eyes, and it indeed looks like smoke.

This story took place at Smoke Hole. I was probably ten or eleven years old. Your great-grandpa Kretoski mainly taught me to fish on the trout streams and on the Shenandoah River. As you read this story, remember the previous story about guardian angels. We were wading in the river and had seen a snake swimming in the water. We were not too concerned, because we thought it was a water snake. Later that morning my dad went to fish upstream, while I stayed in the same vicinity fishing from a large rock in the middle of the river. I was contentedly fishing away. My dad would often leave me alone to fish even on the mighty Shenandoah River, which is very wide and treacherous. Your great-grandma Kretoski would have had a nervous breakdown if she had known about me fishing by myself as a youngster. I was on this rock fishing, and I saw my dad walking rather quickly back down the trail. I was surprised, because it had only been a short period of time. He stood on the edge of the river and said, "Joey, don't move! There is a copper…" That is as far as he got into the sentence. I jumped off that rock into the river like a crazy person. What do you think I saw? Yep, you're right! There was a coiled copperhead snake. I presumed that it was the same snake that we had seen earlier and that it slithered up on that rock without me seeing it. The big question was, "Why didn't the snake strike?" Copperheads are known for their aggressiveness. I had been on that rock fishing, moving around, squatting, etc., and it never bit me. Does this remind you of Daniel in the lion's den? Let me tell you the rest of the story. Dad, who had moved upstream, had a very troubled feeling or impression that something bad was going to happen to his son. That is what prompted him to come to my rescue. He had heeded God's voice.

After I jumped into the water, Dad waded out to me. Now what do you think that copperhead did? It slithered off the rock and swam toward Dad and me. The scene in the water became a little wild, because that snake would not back off. Dad actually broke his pole as he kept that copperhead off from us and from biting us. Yes, that was the same snake that miraculously did not strike me just a few moments earlier. This story is not embellished one iota. People may say that this was just coincidental, but I prefer to think that my guardian angel or God Almighty chose to protect me supernaturally on that rock at Smoke Hole.

There is one more thing that we need to notice about this story. My father was sensitive to the Holy Spirit. When he was prompted by God, he listened and acted. My dear grandchildren, always listen, and be sensitive when God speaks to you. Live close to Jesus so you recognize His voice.

"My sheep hear my voice, and I know them, and they follow me."

JOHN 10:27 (KJV)

A Blast From The Past

My best friend growing up was named Curly. Curly was a great "rabbit dawg." I will tell you several Curly stories soon, but now I will focus on the blast from the past. There was a guy who wanted to rabbit hunt with my dad and me. Somebody in the church asked Dad to take this guy hunting even though we did not know him. My dad always had a "hidden agenda" with people. He always tried to lead people to Jesus and get them to come to church. I am sure this is the main reason that we took this man hunting. However, it almost cost me my life. Curly was running a rabbit, and it turned back to the direction from which it was jumped. The reason I knew this was because Curly's bark began moving toward me. Rabbits will usually return back to the area where they were originally jumped, and that was exactly what this rabbit was doing. I was standing in front of a rather large tree waiting with anticipation. I had my 20-gauge ready and was watching intently. Suddenly I had an intense feeling of foreboding, and fear came over me. I had never had that feeling before, and it scared me. I quickly got behind the tree and hunkered down. Soon after I hunkered down, I heard a shotgun blast, and pellets were hitting the tree that I was hiding behind. If I had stayed where I had been, that shot would have hit me directly. Thank God I heard and listened to God speaking to me. The rabbit had run near the tree where I had been standing. The new guy was not paying attention to where I was and just fired. I can't remember if he hit the rabbit or not. I do remember that when my dad realized what had happened, our hunt was over, and that guy never hunted with us again!

My wonderful grandkids, you always need to listen to the voice of God. Keep your powder dry, and always be careful what you're shooting. Again, there is no debate concerning whether there is a God. God supernaturally warned me with my guardian angel or just by speaking to me. Always listen, and be obedient to the Word of God.

"God is our refuge and strength, a very present help in trouble."
PSALM 46:1 (KJV)

RATTLESNAKE HEAVEN

This story occurred when Grandpa was an adult. Your great-grandpa Kretoski and I were going to fish for smallmouth bass on the South Potomac River near Romney, West Virginia. I had stopped at a bait shop earlier in the week, and they told me the area where we were going was "rattlesnake heaven." On one side of the river there was a steep mountainside, and the owner told me the snakes would come down to sun themselves and to forage for food. When we began walking the railroad tracks, we had our fishing poles, bait, and walking sticks. We were very alert and vigilant. We were going into "rattlesnake heaven" and were rather jittery and jumpy. We walked up the railroad tracks probably four or five miles and then decided to go into the river. When we got off the tracks, there were many downed trees and large rocks. We very nervously moved toward the river poking our walking sticks around rocks and logs. We were expecting to hear a rattlesnake rattle. Both of us were wondering if we really should have taken the risk to fish here, but men sometimes listen to their hearts and not their heads. However, we made it to the river with no snake encounters. Your great-grandpa and I caught several smallies and rock bass. Your great-grandpa was the best fisherman I have ever known, and, yes, he did outfish me on this day. When he went to Heaven, I had never outfished him one single, solitary time. Now, to get back to the story. We fished for two or three hours and began our trek back down the tracks. We were tired, happy, and had lost our attentiveness. We were talking and laughing, and I just happened to look down near my feet. Approximately two feet from us was a rattler sunning itself with his triangular head and slitty eyes hanging over the track. I stopped immediately and hit my dad in the chest with my arm to stop him, and we backed off quickly. That snake curled up quickly and began to rattle. The hair on the back of my neck stood up, and I was full of adrenaline. Dad and I weren't "tree huggers," and we found rocks and killed that snake. We were a bundle of nerves. We placed a larger rock on the snake's head, because the body was still squirming, and I cut the buttons off its tail with a dull knife. When we began our trek again, we were on full alert. We had walked about a mile or so when my dad missed seeing a blue racer snake and stepped right on it. He started hollering and dancing around like a wild thing. It was one of the funniest things I have ever witnessed. Your great-grandpa was usually a very brave man, but he lost it that evening. It was hilarious to see him scream and holler, and do a polka on the tracks! Yes, we finally it made back to the car, but we both probably lost a few years off our lives.

The moral of this story is that we need to stay alert spiritually. Satan has a plan to destroy us and wants to distract us so that we fall into his traps.

"Therefore let him who thinks he stands take heed that he does not fall."

1 CORINTHIANS 10:12 (NASB)

"Watch out! Don't let your hearts be dulled by carousing and drunkenness, and by the worries of this life. Don't let that day catch you unaware."

LUKE 21:34 (NLT)

IT IS MORE BLESSED TO GIVE

This is a story of how Curly became a Kretoski and then became my best friend when I was a boy. My dad had visited a family and told me he had offered to buy their dog from them. He could hear the dog barking while trying to run rabbits behind their home. Curly was less than a year old at this point. These people really liked the dog and refused to sell him. Now if you saw Curly, you probably would not think he looked like a rabbit dog or hound. Dad thought that he was possibly half beagle and half cocker spaniel. He had rather long, curly, and reddish fur—about the color of an Irish setter. Dad was not being malicious, but a few days later, he told me he was going to visit the "Tobaccer Roaders." As a young kid growing up in West Virginia, that expression usually alluded to very poor people who were barely existing and lived in some ramshackle house. That was very true of this family. The reason I remember this is that I actually went with Dad as he visited this family again.

You may be wondering why Great-Grandpa was visiting these people. The answer is rather simple. He felt that everyone needed to be saved and that Jesus was no respecter of people. The poor, rich, uneducated, educated, etc.—everyone needed to find forgiveness and have their lives changed.

To get back to the story, I went with Dad into that dilapidated house, which was dirty and bombarded with flies. Dad was very kind and considerate as he talked with them. The wife was trying to be reciprocal and offered us something to drink and a piece of pie. Dad received it graciously and prayed that God would bless and sanctify the pie. With all the flies and dirt, it surely needed to be sanctified! I forced the pie down and watched my dad minister to these people and then pray for them before we left. I also watched my dad sneak a twenty-dollar bill under the pie plate. Twenty dollars was a lot of money to these people, but Great-Grandpa just wanted to help them and lead them to Jesus. I don't know if they had a phone or borrowed the neighbors' phone, but when we got home we had a message that they wanted us to have the red dog. We went back and picked up Curly, and he became my best friend and developed into a great rabbit dog. He lived to be thirteen years old, and if any dog deserved to go to Heaven, it was Curly.

I will write more stories in the future with Curly as the main character, but for now, never forget that it is always more blessed to give than to receive.

CRAZY DREAMS

Your grandpa did some rather ridiculous things back when he was a young kid. He had some rather wild dreams. I will write about two of them. When these stories took place, we lived in Bell, California, and I was probably around seven or eight years old. I wanted to fly, and in my imagination I could see myself flying like a bird. I made some wings out of cardboard and really thought that if I flapped my wings hard and fast enough, I would soar. I fitted those wings on my arms and went to one end of the front porch. This porch was rather long and had a few steps at the end. I took off running, and when I got to the other end of the porch, I launched myself into the air, flapping my wings furiously. I knew I was going to fly like a bird! The problem was that I flew like a dead bird. I crashed into the asphalt and did the best belly-flopper in the world. I bruised and battered my face, chest, arms, and legs terribly. I was also bleeding rather profusely. The worst thing was that my dream died with my crash landing. I was a rather devastated little boy, and the scabs all over my body were a reminder for many days.

When I look back, it is easy to see that your grandpa was rather goofy and impulsive at times. In the next scenario I jumped off a house. Have you ever watched Mary Poppins or maybe a cartoon when someone jumped off a building and then floated to the ground, because they used an umbrella as a parachute? One more time I allowed my imagination and my dream to fly to cloud my rational thinking. Well, kids, I think you know exactly what I did. I don't remember how I even got on that roof, but I got there. I went to the edge of the peak, got my umbrella in place, and jumped. I was fulfilling my dreams. I was going to float like a butterfly in the wind and eventually have a peaceful landing. My dream may have lasted half a second. When I jumped, the umbrella went inside out in a flash, and I hit the ground with a major crash. Miraculously, my body was bruised but not broken. My inner spirit may have been bruised and battered, but not broken. I still had dreams and expectations, but just became a little more careful of how they were accomplished. Also, I am thankful that I only jumped off a one-story house!

Grandkids, you will also have dreams. Some of them will work out, while others won't. That is just how life is. When your dreams crash, pick yourself up, and learn from the experience. It is normal to struggle emotionally after a failure, but after a while you have to pick yourself up and keep living and dreaming! Always be malleable, and allow God to lead and direct your life as well as your dreams!

"Trust in the LORD with all your heart, and lean not on your own understanding; In all your ways acknowledge Him, and He shall direct your paths."

PROVERBS 3:5–6 (NKJV)

Timmy Put Two Fish
In The Bucket

This next story is not about me but about my nephew, Timmy, and Great-Grandpa. This story is true, amazing, and unembellished, to the best of my knowledge. My dad, your great-grandpa, was a great fisherman. He caught more fish than any man I ever knew. He caught fish even when other people weren't catching fish. When he got older, he never stopped fishing, but his main quest was bluegills. He not only enjoyed catching them but enjoyed eating them. Even to this day, we still fry fish in exactly the same way that Great-Grandpa and Great-Grandma taught us. Almost every time I sink my teeth into a bluegill or smallmouth bass, I have pleasant thoughts about my parents and our family fish fry.

Great-Grandpa loved to take his grandkids bluegill fishing with him. After they caught them, they helped him clean them. On this particular fishing excursion near Arthurdale, West Virginia, Timmy and Great-Grandpa went bluegill fishing. They had probably caught around twenty-five fish, and my dad asked Timmy how many fish he had caught. I won't say Timmy lied, but he definitely embellished the number of fish that he put in the bucket. Great-Grandpa had observed Timmy only putting two fish in the bucket. My understanding of the story is that he told Timmy he would not catch another fish until he was honest. He also began singing a little song that said, "Timmy put two fish in the bucket."

Knowing my dad the way that I did, I can almost guarantee that he continued to sing his little ditty often. Dad continued to catch fish, and Timmy never got a single bite. I believe this went on for close to half an hour—Dad singing, catching fish consistently, and Timmy only getting a sunburn. Finally, Timmy blurted out the truth that he had actually caught only two fish. What do you think happened? You're right! His bobber immediately went down, and Timmy put another fish in the bucket.

Great-Grandpa must have had great faith in his God to make such a bold statement to Timmy: "You will not catch another fish until you're truthful." Timmy was taught a lesson about honesty, but also that there is a supernatural God who can control even the fish. I might tell you also that Great-Grandpa prayed every time he went fishing. He literally asked God to help him catch fish, because he knew that the Heavenly Father would give him the desires of his heart.

This story has become legendary with the Kretoski family. When you kids grow older, get married, and have kids of your own, I hope you tell this story to your families.

"Do not lie to each other, since you have taken off your old self with its practices."

COLOSSIANS 3:9 (NIV)

PRAYING FOR OUR
PROTECTION

Grandma and Grandpa had only been married for a few years when they traveled to Texas to visit Great-Grandma and Great-Grandpa who were pastoring a church in the Panhandle. We decided to take a couple of days to visit Mexico. No, we could not speak Spanish and did not really know much about the culture. We were told that when you park your car that you had better pay somebody to watch it, or it might get stripped down. In other words, someone may steal the tires and anything valuable. We crossed the International Bridge into Mexico, and I must have taken a wrong turn, because we soon ended up in a very rough section of town. The roads were narrow, and people drove carelessly. I found a parking place and parked as quickly as possible, right in front of a bar. Anyway, we both needed to use the restroom, so we walked into this sleazy joint. I communicated that we needed to use the bathrooms, and they showed us where to go. They were dirty and stinky, and I was worrying about Grandma. She was an awfully good-looking woman, and those guys did not look too trustworthy. The adrenalin was flowing, and I was ready to rumble. Finally she came out of the nasty bathroom. I then acted like I knew what I was doing and offered a man some money to watch our car, an almost spanking, brand-new Ford Fiesta. We gave him some money and very nervously left and went shopping. We did not shop very long but had several people, including children, trying to sell us whiskey and cigarettes. We also saw a person eating out of the trash. These circumstances were such a cultural shock. We eventually made it back to the car (which had not been stripped), gave the guy more money, and headed back to the "good ole U.S.A." We were trying to find the International Bridge, and a bus got on our tail and wanted to pass us on the narrow roads. I pulled over as quickly as possible and let it get past us. We were very thankful when we crossed over into the U.S.A. but also realized how well we really lived. We were pretty poor by American standards but were rich compared to those very poor Mexicans.

We then drove to San Antonio, which is where the story takes a turn. We pulled into a motel and got a room, which was no big deal. The problem was that I got a very uneasy feeling. I had a genuine fear for myself and my wife. The first and the last time that has ever happened to me was walking into that motel room. I cautiously checked out the room with Grandma staying close behind me. I walked into the bathroom and checked behind the shower curtain, and everything seemed okay, at least until I saw that the bathroom window was open. I quickly shut and locked it. I checked under the bed again as well as the door locks several times, and, of course, the bathroom window. My mind was in turmoil. Was that uneasiness and fear my imagination, or was it a warning from God? It took a while, but we finally went to sleep, and I did not have the most restful night. We got up in the morning and drove back to Wichita Falls. Remember that this was years before there were cell phones, and we had not communicated with my folks. When we arrived, Mom and Dad met us on the porch and had very concerned looks on their faces. Mom, almost frantically, was asking if we were okay and what had happened last night. The previous night at the exact same time we had arrived at the motel, God put a fear and dread in the hearts of your great-grandparents, and they prayed intensely for our protection. The fear and anxiety that I felt was actually God warning me and Grandma. I have wondered many, many times since then what would have happened if my parents had not listened to the voice of God and immediately prayed for us.

Grandkids, Satan wants us to get so busy with life or so involved with our electronics that we don't hear His voice and lose our spiritual sensitivity. I remember being at camp meeting, and the evangelist was preaching with God's anointing. There were five teenage boys sitting directly in front of me, not hearing one single word. Why? They were all using their cell phones, and it wasn't for Scripture! May you always be sensitive to the Spirit and hear his voice. Who knows? Maybe your prayers will save the life or protect one of your friends or family.

"My sheep hear my voice, and I know them, and they follow me."

JOHN 10:27 (KJV)

CRAZY ANGER

This is going to be another Curly story. I really am not too proud of myself in this story but decided that sometimes you've got to write about the good and the bad. This story is going to be about when Grandpa allowed his anger to overwhelm him. Before I continue with this story, I just want to talk to you a little bit about anger. Anger is a very controversial subject. Some people think that a person can reach a spiritual state where they no longer have anger issues, while others espouse that anger is always an issue and that you just can't help but lose your temper. I really don't agree with either of those. I think there are different stages of anger, but normally anger is just a natural emotion that arises when we are hurt or aggravated. There are times when we may feel anger when we see people treated unjustly, or maybe a situation was handled unfairly. If your brother or sister punches you in the back, you are probably going to feel anger. Does this give you the right to punch them back? NO!! This is rather simple, but hopefully you're getting the point.

Grandpa thinks that people can control their anger if they choose. I have talked with many people who say that they can't help themselves. I don't necessarily believe them. They allow their emotions and anger to be their dictator or to control them. I once had a boy tell me that his psychiatrist or psychologist told him that he could not control his anger. He was rather proud that he had done ten thousand dollars' worth of damage in a classroom. He was very upset when I told him he had been

23

lied to and that he had the capacity to control himself. What do you think happened a few weeks later? The boy became very angry in my office and tried to "trash" it. He was quickly and carefully incapacitated by myself and another staff, and was screaming that he could not help himself. In a very respectful manner, I told him that he was accountable for his actions and attitudes. This kid controlled his temper for many months after this episode and learned to think before acting. I realize that people who have been abused in any way are probably more volatile, but with God's help and right counsel, they, too, can gain more control of themselves.

Grandpa never liked to be bullied or to see another person bullied. I was in fifth or sixth grade playing basketball on the school courts. While I was playing, a group of high school kids came to the court and kicked me off. Yes, I was angry, and I called them nasty names, but I let my anger carry me over a cliff. I decided if I could not play, then neither could they. I went home and put Curly on a leash and took him back to the court. I also took my Barlow knife out of my pocket. I kept Curly on the leash but sicced him on them and then started slashing at them with my knife. Curly was growling and trying to bite them. I just got crazy. I would not allow those kids to play basketball. They thought I went "psycho," and they may have been correct. I don't think I have ever been quite that crazy before or after. I said some really bad things to those boys and told them never to push me off the courts again. I then walked home feeling quite powerful that I just terrorized several teenage boys with the help of Curly. Those kids never bullied me again. They still pushed the younger kids off the court but never me. I always got to play after that.

I have thought about that many, many times over the decades, and I still don't quite understand what made me snap, but it did scare me a little bit. I was not saved when this occurred, and even as a young boy, I realized that without God in my heart, I had potential to do some really bad things. I always wanted to please my parents and God. God used this crazy situation to draw me to Him. Did I have to get crazy with those boys? Absolutely not! I allowed my emotions to take over my thinking, and my rational mind and heart were blindsided. Satan knows our weaknesses and our natural tendencies. It will take good choices on our parts and God's Spirit in our hearts for us to overcome sin and evil. Give your heart and life to Jesus while you are young.

Curly was not only my best friend; he was also my protector. Curly would always get aggressive if anyone "messed" with Grandpa.

"I can do all things through Christ who strengthens me."

MOTORCYCLE LONGING

This story will probably be one of the oddest stories that you will ever read, but I promise that every word is true. There are a lot of questions concerning love. Can a person fall in love at first sight? Can a person have such wonderful chemistry that they know that this is Mr. or Mrs. Right? Could a person actually be drawn to another person though they don't even know they exist? I may be old, but I surely don't have all the answers, and the older I get, the fewer answers I have.

It was the summer between my junior and senior years in high school, so I would have been seventeen years old. That summer I was riding my motorcycle to Big Rapids, Michigan, to help an older gentleman lay blocks, so for several days I rode from Evart to Big Rapids. The only problem that I encountered was that when I drove by a certain house, I had a longing to meet the person who lived there. I would slow my cycle down and try to see into the backyard, and then I would stare down the driveway. I tried to conjure up excuses to stop there but just could not provoke my imagination enough to find even a slightly rational excuse. One time I slowed my cycle down and almost pulled into the driveway. I was going to ask for a drink of water. The people who lived in that house would have thought that I had lost my mind, and I'm not sure that I hadn't. I never stopped, but I always wondered about the inhabitants of that house on Chippewa Lake Road every single time I went by. A year had gone by, and a group from a church in Big Rapids came to Pineview to sing and to minister to the Pineview kids. I began to observe the singers and became totally stunned. There singing was the most beautiful Christian girl upon whom I had ever laid my eyes. When she smiled, she lit up the whole yard. I was mesmerized for the remainder of the evening. One thing for certain is that I had to get to know this person. I had not felt that much longing in about a year. I don't remember how it all happened, but I did have the opportunity to get acquainted with her. I may have acted all cool and collected outwardly, but when that beautiful girl smiled at me, my heart melted, and my pulse rate skyrocketed. I had to get to know her better. I overheard her talking with her girlfriend about going to the fair in Big Rapids. Guess what? My best friend, Greg, and I decided to go to the fair in Big Rapids, also. What a coincidence! We met up with that girl, her sister, and a friend. I don't remember anything about the fair that night, but it was getting close to midnight, and the next day was Sunday. We told them we had to leave, but that girl invited Greg and me to her home for something to eat. We just followed their car. They turned onto Chippewa Lake Road, and I did not think much about it. We traveled for a few miles, and we got closer and closer to Chippewa Lake. We were coming to "that house" where I had had a longing to meet someone. Suddenly the blinker on their car began to light, and my mind was going absolutely wacky, because they were turning into "that" driveway. Greg probably thought I was going nuts when I kept repeating, "I can't believe this!" What I did not know is that we had just pulled into your grandma's driveway!

This sounds too crazy to be true, but it is. I am not certain that God has one special person picked out for you to marry, but I am rather certain he did for me. Always be careful whom you date, and don't just jump into marriage. Besides getting saved, whom you marry is the most important decision you will ever make.

"He who finds a wife finds a good thing."

PROVERBS 18:22 (NKJV)

"But seek ye first the kingdom of God, and His righteousness; and all these things shall be added unto you."

MATTHEW 6:33 (KJV)

When Grandpa Almost Died

Years ago when I was little boy, we moved to Southern California for a few years. My father had been saved for only a couple of years, and it was a time for him to learn the Word and to mature as a Christian. It was during this time when my parents' faith was tested. Their only son, your grandpa, became deathly sick at three and a half years old. Some of this story I actually remember, and other parts were verbally passed down to me. It was a Sunday morning when I woke up with my whole body severely bloated. My parents knew that I was very sick and immediately got me medical care. I don't really know if I was taken to the doctor or to the emergency room. I was diagnosed with a severe case of nephritis. This is a kidney disease that makes it very difficult to urinate. It can cause blood clots, which lead to sudden strokes, and the prognosis was very poor. The doctor told your great-grandparents that I would probably die, or if I lived, I would have a very limited life. I would always need care, could never get tired or play sports, and would just live a semi-vegetative life. Of course, my parents and three sisters were distraught. I was placed in Hollywood Children's Hospital where my parents were told that I would get the best care in the world. My mother spent every day with me, and your great-great-grandma Davis came from West Virginia to take care of the girls. My mother told me that I just languished and really made no progress. The doctor did not give my folks much hope. My parents' only recourse was to pray, and my dad asked every Christian he knew to pray for his boy. I lay in that hospital bed for many days, and people just kept praying. Dad told me that one day a Christian friend came up to him and told him not to worry about his son anymore, because God had revealed to him while praying for me that I would be healed. Dad told me he initially reacted negatively toward this man. He said, "Don't tell me this unless you are certain." The man was very kind and reassured Dad that God had spoken to him, and he was confident that I would be healed. The man gave Dad one requirement, and that was that he would raise me to serve the Lord. Dad believed his friend and left very encouraged. Though Dad was a young Christian, he had faith in his God. It was soon after this that God totally restored and healed my body. It was not gradual, but instantaneous. I was normal! I was overactive! The hospital staff tried to calm me down. Somebody bought me a dart gun, and I can still remember shooting the nurses. They told my parents I could not get tired. I was even carried to the bathroom. How crazy can you get? I knew that I was okay. After seventeen days I was released from the hospital with strict rules. I could not get tired or play outside, and I was not even allowed to walk. I was carried everywhere. Guess what? I learned to sneak. As soon as the room cleared out, I ran around like a wild thing. I was one energetic little boy. I was healed! I did take advantage of the rides and became a spoiled brat. Everyone gave me everything I wanted. It was probably hard not to when everyone thought I was going to die. I was taken to many doctor's appointments after I came home. Many doctors found it difficult to believe that I had been touched by Jesus.

I have been strong and active for most of my life. I played little league as a boy and played sports in high school. I stayed quite active until my body got older, but I still enjoy hunting and fishing.

Grandkids, never ever lose faith or trust in an all-powerful God. You will face situations that you will not understand, but keep praying and believing. Never, ever give up!

"And the prayer of faith shall save the sick, and the Lord shall raise him up."

JAMES 5:15A (KJV)

30

Accused

Our family attended church camp every summer. This story took place in Michigan at the United Holiness Camp when I was around thirteen years old. This camp had a boys' dorm that probably had twenty-five or thirty bunks, if my memory serves me correctly. Why they let us boys stay in the dorm without adult supervision is beyond me. That is a recipe for chaos! There was a man who slept next to the dorm in a tent who tried to supervise us, but nobody slept inside the dorm. Once I wired his vertical tent zipper to the two horizontal zippers and pulled up his tent stakes. It was funny then but is not too funny now, as I think back. We took advantage of this lack of supervision to the fullest. The bell would ring for everyone to be in their rooms and to have lights out. We would make sure we were all in the dorm after the bell, because our friend who slept in the tent would do a dorm check. We were quiet and compliant, at least for a short period of time. Then we would begin to get loud, tell jokes, snap each other with towels, etc. I remember pouring water or pop into another guy's shoes and spreading peanut butter on a guy's bedding. Most of us were bad, and I was really bad. I remember catching frogs and sneaking into a cabin where three or four girls were staying. While they were in the evening service, I put several frogs into their sleeping bags. I wanted them to scream like wild women when they went to bed. What I did not know is that those girls were leaving after the service and rolled up those sleeping bags and took them home with frogs

31

in them. To this day I don't know whether I should feel guilty or what, but I laughed like an idiot then. Can you imagine the stench that seeped from those sleeping bags, after they got home?

There were several boys who would sneak out of the dorm at night, and I was always one of them. We loved being chased by the "camp cops." It was a blast! They could not catch us young guys. One time I climbed into a tree next to another dorm with my pockets full of rocks. A rather young and brash "camp cop" who was also a preacher stood next to my tree. His head was rotating back and forth as he tried to detect movement. He was on high alert, and I was loving every second of it. I would take a rock out of my pocket and toss it about twenty feet from him. He would move in that direction quickly, and then I would toss another rock. He would run over there. I threw several rocks, and he never looked up. I was only twelve or fifteen feet above him. I nearly fell out of the tree as I was laughing so hard inwardly and trying to be quiet. This brings us to the serious part of this story. The dorm supervisor was rather irritated with us boys for being loud, crazy, and leaving the dorm. On this particular evening I promised him I would not leave the dorm after the bell. This is crazy, but every single boy sneaked out that night except for me. I may have been rotten and mischievous, but I was honest. I never left the dorm. The "camp cops" were doing the usual "cat and mouse" thing, and eventually everyone came back to the dorm. The dorm supervisor came into the dorm and turned the lights on. You probably know whom he spotted and whom he confronted. Yes, you are right—your grandpa! He was telling me how I had promised not to leave and called me a liar. In retrospect I really don't blame him for reacting like he did, but as a young teenager, I was highly offended when he called me a liar. I tried to argue my case, but his mind was made up. I was a liar. I asked one of my friends to go get my dad. In a few minutes my dad walked into the dorm in a calm manner. He looked at me, then at the dorm supervisor and asked what the problem was. He was told by the dorm supervisor that I had broken my promise and left the dorm. Most dads would have reacted and accused their sons and possibly destroyed their spirits in the process. My dad calmly asked me, "Joey, did you leave the dorm?" I told him I did not leave the dorm. My dad, with little, if any, emotion, turned to the dorm supervisor and said, "Joey did not leave the dorm," and calmly walked out. It was over, and he had trusted me. Short and sweet, but one of the most powerful experiences a teenage boy could ever experience. My dad had one more time affirmed his son. Wow, I would have run through a block wall for my dad! One more time I was so proud to be my father's son. Probably some of those boys were rather envious of me, because few fathers would ever be that sensitive and trusting.

Why had my father, your great-grandfather, so readily believed me? I had never, ever lied to my father, and we had an indestructible trust in each other. Yes, we could have broken the trust by being deceitful or dishonest, but we never did. Not even once!

I might add a small tidbit to this story. Grandkids, someday when you have your own children, do not ever forget how tender and delicate their spirits will be. Their wills are normally strong and tough, but that inner spirit can easily be offended. Never just jump to conclusions with your children. Be strong but never disrespectful.

"A good name is rather to be chosen than great riches."

PROVERB 22:1 (KJV)

"In the same way, let your light shine before others, so that they may see your good works and give glory to your Father who is in Heaven."

MATTHEW 5:16 (ESV)

WILD BANSHEE

I was preaching at my first church, a small holiness church in Elkins, West Virginia. Elkins is a beautiful area surrounded by mountains and some pristine trout streams nearby. I had also shot several deer on Bickle Knob. My family and I moved to Elkins without ever visiting the church or parsonage. I'm not complaining, but the property had been neglected for a long time. Several of the church basement windows were broken. There were walls in the church that had holes in them, and the lawn in the backyard had not been mowed for a long time. When I questioned about the holes in the walls, I was told that teenagers did it. When asked why they were allowed, the person asked, "How do you stop them?" Maybe I was brash, but I was thinking that over my dead body would they do that! There were a lot of other issues, such as raw sewage flowing into the crawl space under the parsonage. It had been disconnected for who knows how long before we arrived. We weren't aware of it either for a while. Is it any wonder that Betsy and Joey were often sick for several months after we moved in? Joey ended up in the hospital rather sick with bronchitis and croup for a few days. My good friend, Ray, will never know how much I appreciated him after we reconnected the sewage pipes. I wasn't much help, because I was constantly gagging and trying not to vomit. Ray had not been saved yet, but I remember what he said to me after we were done "wallering" in that mess: "I think you are a keeper." Isn't it funny how we remember the little things people say? The property was a mess, and the church's reputation in the community was very negligible. The church had had many issues in the past.

You're probably wondering why Grandpa and Grandma ever moved there. The main reason was that we felt God called us there. We were not one bit discouraged. We loved the few church people and were beginning to love the community. It was difficult getting acquainted in the community because of the church's reputation. I would take Betsy out with me as I visited. She was so adorable that she opened many doors for me. They did not like the preacher initially, but they could not resist the charming little four-year-old Betsy. I am not going to spend a long time telling you about our time at Elkins, but things did progress nicely. People started attending and found Jesus, the grounds got fixed up, we started a Christian school, and the community actually accepted me as the community pastor.

I am going to tell you a little story that happened soon after I arrived at Elkins. The youth in the community had little respect for that church or God in general. One Sunday morning as I was leading the service, the most delinquent teenager in the community entered the church. He started screaming like a wild banshee and ran out of the church. Everyone sat in the pews astonished. I asked someone to lead the service, as I also ran out of the church. I chased that boy down the middle of the road and finally apprehended him. He was rather dumbfounded that I would run him down. I put my arm around his shoulders and gave him two options. He could take me to his parents, and I would explain what just happened. I was rather certain he was scared that he would get the tar beat out of him. His second option was to follow me back to church and sit on the front pew until I dismissed. I was rather amused at the shocked faces of the crowd when I walked in with him. They knew all about this kid. He sat there quietly and respectfully while I preached and dismissed. His mother actually attended my church for a while, and I never told her about this incident. After this wild episode, we never had any more problems with youth in the community. They learned to like and respect the new preacher. It also helped that I would play basketball with them up at the school and had great rapport with them. God can take a bad situation and use it for good.

Grandkids, there will be good things and bad things that happen to you. Satan will try to obstruct your walk with Christ when bad things happen. Your great-grandfather would say, "Never cast your confidence away." Try to be patient and allow God to bring something good from negative situations.

> "And we know that all things work together for good to them that love God, to them who are the called according to His purpose."
>
> ROMANS 8:28 (KJV)

BRIDGE JUMPING

Grandpa learned to swim at an early age, probably at around seven years old. I remember jumping and diving off the high dive at Bell High School in California. I also would swim out into the Pacific Ocean and belly-surf the waves in to shore as a young kid. Great-Grandma Kretoski would have been fretting and stewing if she'd had any idea about some of the crazy things her little boy did. I never had a fear of water and even greatly enjoyed tubing wild rapids on the Shenandoah River. I lived at Pineview Homes, a youth home in Evart, Michigan, for three years as an older teenager. I was a staff kid, but there were plenty of people who thought I was one of the residents. In the summer we used to take the guys swimming over to Hersey Bridge on the Muskegon River. I loved diving and jumping off the lower rail, which was quite a distance above the river. I was told it was seventeen feet to the water. One day I dove in, and the pressure from hitting water pushed my cutoffs clear to my ankles. I thought I was going to drown before I drifted around the bend and pulled them up. My problem came when jumping off the top railing. Several Pineview boys, as well as Paul and Greg, jumped off the top rail many times. I even watched Greg dive off the top of the bridge. I was told it was approximately forty feet from the top rail to the water. This is one time your grandpa was fearful. Believe me, I was rather embarrassed about my anxiety and was challenged and harassed by my friends to climb to the top and jump off. My youthful pride eventually overcame my fear, and I climbed to the top rail with an inner dread that I tried to cover with a fake bravado. After I stood up on the rail, I was hoping that no one could see my knees shaking and quaking. Grandkids, I can't tell you how many times I counted to three before I jumped. When I jumped, it was a "rush" and very exhilarating. Did I ever jump off the top again? Yes, several times. Did I ever lose all my fear and anxiety? Not completely, but mostly.

I really did desire to jump off the top rail, but the main reason I did was peer pressure. Jumping off the bridge was scary for me, but it was not wrong or sinful. There will be times when you may be challenged to do something out of your comfort zone. It might be a good thing. Sometimes, with anxiety, you must just do it to overcome it. There will be times as you grow up when you will be pressured to do things that are sinful and wrong. I remember one time when I was a freshman in high school, I was riding around town with some friends after a basketball game. They told me that they were going to get someone to buy them beer and then party, and asked if I wanted to drink with them. I had never been confronted with this type of peer pressure before. I had to make a choice of whether I wanted to please my friends or my parents. Did I really want to please my God? I was trying my best to live a clean Christian life. I just loved my parents too much to hurt them. I am not saying it was easy, but with God's help I asked my friends to take me home. I was still their friend but never a close friend. God gave me better friends. That experience made me a better and stronger person. There will always be peer pressure and temptation, but there will be times you will have to say "no" and maybe run away like a wild rabbit.

Another thing that we need to be aware of is that Satan probably knows our weaknesses. He will lay traps and temptations before us, and we will fall if we aren't careful. The number one key to overcoming is to live close to God. Read the Bible, pray, meditate on God's goodness, worship Him, and be busy in kingdom work.

"This I say then, walk in the Spirit, and ye shall not fulfil the lust of the flesh."

GALATIANS 5:16 (KJV)

"God is faithful, and He will not let you be tempted beyond your ability, but with the temptation He will also provide the way of escape, that you may be able to endure it."

1 CORINTHIANS 10:13B (ESV)

FRENZY

The word frenzy means a state or period of uncontrolled excitement or wild behavior. This story took place around 2011 or so. Sam and I were fishing for river smallmouth bass in September. In the fall most fish will begin to prepare for winter and will start biting better. Sometimes, you find the fish when they are in a feeding "frenzy." I remember wet-wading the river once and had twenty-one straight bites. I never moved more than ten feet that evening and caught fifty-eight fish. That was a rather monumental number to me. I once saw my dad catch forty-eight smallmouth one afternoon on the Shenandoah River. Your grandpa almost stopped fishing at number forty-seven, because I just did not want to beat my dad. My memories of fishing with your great-grandpa are very special to me. Life was very busy for him, and when we went fishing, things slowed down. We talked about God. We talked about important things between a dad and son. I asked him questions, and he tried to always answer them wisely. It was then that he opened up a "teensy bit" concerning his upbringing. It was hard for him to talk about certain things. He told me several times that he wanted me to be raised differently than he had been. Dad did talk with me more about it when I was an adult, but it was never easy for him. I actually got emotional while fishing that evening, just reliving good memories. I was also wondering if Dad was watching from Heaven. He was extremely competitive, but if he could see me, I think he would have been cheering me on. I did catch fifty-eight bass that evening and enjoyed myself immensely. I did catch more than that several times after that.

Sam and I put the boat in and went to a favorite hole. From the very first cast we started catching fish—one after another, double after double. A double is when both people in the boat have fish on at the same time. We moved to a different spot and kept catching fish after fish. We would move to another area, and the same thing happened—fish after fish and double after double. We were actually amazed and astounded that we just kept catching fish. It was epic! We caught 232 smallmouth bass in three hours. That is a fish to the boat every forty-six and a half seconds. What a blast! What a memory! We will probably never catch fish like that again, but it sure is a nice thought that we might. A normal evening of fishing would probably net about thirty bass. To be successful you've got to keep fishing. You have to keep casting. You have to have your bait in the water.

Fishing is kind of like life. Sometimes life is just wonderful with great experiences, but at other times it is rather routine. You just do what you normally do and put one foot in front of the other. If you stay consistent and focused, you will reach your goals and maybe accomplish more than you thought possible. Every once in a while you will have a wonderful and magnificent day. The most important thing is to find God's will for your life and to live for Him. Give God your all. Give Him your whole heart. That is the key to a fulfilling life!

Jesus said, "Follow me, and I will make you fishers of men."

MATTHEW 4:19 (KJV)

Catching a big smallmouth bass is a blast, but nothing is more wonderful than leading a person to Christ! Keep catching fish, but catch some people, also.

RED FOX

This story took place when we lived in Mecosta, Michigan. It was during the late seventies or early eighties. This is one of those stories that seems to be very outlandish, but don't allow doubt to enter your mind. Every word of this story is true, and hopefully it will be a reminder of how great and caring God is. He probably has a sense of humor, also.

Michigan winters can be long, cold, snowy, and harsh. Michigan had some very bad winters in the late seventies, with blizzards, snow drifts that were incredibly high, roads that were totally impassable, and white-outs where a person could barely see.

We had had another rough winter. It was March, and spring was due to arrive. There was a major problem at the Kretoski residence. We heated our home with wood, and our supply of wood was almost depleted. You are probably wondering why we just did not pick up the phone and call someone to bring us wood. The problem was that we did not have any extra money for wood, and we just did not want to ask somebody for money. Grandma and Grandpa did the only thing we knew to do—pray! We thought that a rick of wood would get us through the winter. We prayed specifically for $35.00. That was the cost of a rick of wood back then. Now, Grandkids, this is where the story gets a bit crazy. We expected someone to give us the money or to get a surprise letter in the mail. The wood pile was getting lower, and we kept praying.

We really were trusting in God. We weren't walking around looking like hound dogs and feeling sorry for ourselves. We just had faith that God would answer our prayers when He was ready. Your great-grandpa and I went rabbit hunting at Chippewa Lake. Michigan's rabbit season goes to the end of March. I don't remember if we shot any rabbits or not, but I do remember there were several inches of snow on the ground. We walked up a little knoll and both of us stopped in our tracks. There were hundreds and possibly thousands of pine trees on this eighty acres, but our focus was on one tree. Was it dead? Was it alive? We walked closer and closer. There at the base of that tree was a dead red fox. It was not lying on its side where it would have been next to impossible to see, but it was standing upright on four legs. It was astounding! I have never seen a dead animal die upright. It was frozen like a statue. There were no cuts or mange on the fox. It had died standing up with no blemishes on it. What are the odds of finding one fox, standing in front of one pine tree, on eighty acres, with several inches of snow on the ground? What are the odds of finding a needle in a haystack? There would have been very similar odds with this fox and that needle. I hauled that fox to the car. I did not skin it; I did not do anything to it. I took that fox to a guy who handled furs and who had a reputation of being rather stingy. I knew that he was going to try to rip me off, but he was the only person I knew who was a fur handler. The first thing he did was criticize, because the fox wasn't skinned. Then he looked at me and asked if I would be willing to take $35.00 for that fox, because that's all that he would give me. I nonchalantly told him, "Yes, I'll take it." Man, inside I almost screamed and hollered like a mad man. I thought my heart was going to burst in my chest. When I got in my car, the dam broke. All I could do was cry and thank God for His goodness. He had answered our prayers for wood!

Grandkids, never lose faith in an all-knowing and all-powerful God. Whatever you encounter in life and no matter how bleak or horrible it looks, never quit believing or lose faith. Never stop praying, and never, ever give up.

"For He has said, I will in no way leave you, neither will I in any way forsake you."

HEBREWS 13:5B (WEB)

What a wonderful promise that all of God's children can claim!

Asking Forgiveness

This is another true story, but it has a very sensitive subject—forgiveness. There are many and varied opinions on this subject, but, as usual, Grandpa has his opinion, also. We would like to think that the perpetrator or the person who is guilty would need to initiate the forgiveness process, but that normally only happens occasionally. Usually it is the person who is hurt or offended that initiates the forgiving. People have a real tendency to carry a grudge or, as the Bible says, to have "a root of bitterness." The only way that Grandpa knew to find real healing was to forgive. Corrie ten Boom said, "Forgiveness is to set a prisoner free, and to realize the prisoner was you." That may be hard to understand now, but someday you will. There is one thing for certain and that is that you will need to forgive others. Maybe you will understand this better if I just tell the story.

When I was twelve years old, your great-grandfather began to pastor a church in Michigan. I loved West Virginia, and it was a very hard move for me. I may love Michigan now, but at the time all I saw were swamps, mosquitoes, and that the people talked funny. I missed the mountains and Southern accents. I missed the trout streams and the Shenandoah River. Michigan people actually drank tea with no sugar. That was crazy!

When we left West Virginia, I was upset with a couple of families in the church, because I had seen them disrespect my dad in a Sunday evening service. They made some untrue accusations and invited my dad to the altar. Instead of my dad overreacting and putting those people in their places, he displayed a humble and Godly spirit. I remember this situation very clearly. My dad stood up and told the congregation that if there was anything in his heart that was sinful, He wanted God to show him. He asked the people to pray with him as he went to the altar. The problem was that the son was not as kind and benevolent as his father. They had just disrespected and hurt the man whom I respected the most. Anger took root in my heart. When we moved to Michigan, the anger moved with me. I allowed this anger to fester until I became bitter inside my heart. Had I done anything wrong? Yes, and no. I did not do any-thing to anybody, but I did allow anger to take root in my heart. I was doing my best to live a Christian life, but when I thought of those two families, there was nothing but ugliness that filled my mind and heart. I made excuses in my mind. They should have never treated my dad like that. I did not think about this often, but when I did, it was not pretty. I was bitter toward those church people. Grandkids, whom was I hurting? Only myself. Anger and bitterness will eat you alive if you don't forgive and release it. Nevertheless, two years had passed, and we were visiting my sister in West Virginia. I was now in ninth grade and fourteen years old. I was attending the Sunday evening service at my dad's old church. Guess who was in the service? You're right one more time. Those people! I was sitting near the back trying to ignore the small, quiet voice of God stirring my heart. My heart was pounding, and I knew exactly what I was supposed to do. The altar call was given, and I went to the altar trying to satisfy God. One good man prayed very loudly and beat the tar out of my back. He was a very good man and was only trying to encourage me. After praying at the altar, I went back to my pew, but there was no peace. The trouble was that I had not fully obeyed God. A few people had testi-fied, and I knew what I had to do. My heart was pounding, and God was speaking directly to me. It was not audible, but I could hear Him loudly and clearly. If I was going to release this bitterness, I had to obey God and do it His way. It was not easy, but I obeyed one hundred percent. A very proud young man needed to humble himself and be obedient to God.

God is patient, but we always need to listen and obey. If we don't, it will hinder our relationship with God and eventually possibly even destroy our relationship. I stood up and walked to the front of the church. I did not mention names and circumstances, but I did tell them I had become bitter over a previous situation in the church. I asked the church to forgive me. I obeyed God and released that nasty bitterness in my heart. The prisoner had been set free, and I had been that prisoner. I was finally free after two years. I felt clean and at peace.

Grandkids, you will be hurt and offended several times during your lifetime. It is going to happen. Even people who love you may hurt you. Don't allow your hurt and anger to take root in your heart. Don't retaliate, and don't hold a grudge. Anger and bitterness will destroy you—body, soul, and spirit. Always forgive, and move on.

"And be ye kind one to another, tenderhearted, forgiving one another, even as God for Christ's sake hath forgiven you."

 EPHESIANS 4:32 (KJV)

"Forbearing one another, and forgiving one another, if any man have a quarrel against any: even as Christ forgave you, so also do ye."

COLOSSIANS 3:13 (KJV)

Surrender

Grandkids, there will be times in your life when you just don't know what to do or where to go. These times can be very frustrating, because we want things when we want them. Your generation is probably worse than mine. I call it the microwave generation. Most people want what they want immediately with little or no patience. Oftentimes, people allow their anxiety levels to soar and never take time to pray or really trust God for guidance. We become like Peter walking on the water during the storm. Instead of continuing to look to Jesus, we begin to see the wild waves. The waves would be symbolic of the bad circumstances with which we are confronted. Peter would have drowned if Jesus had not rescued him. There comes a point where God wants us to surrender to His will. He does not want His children to be willful and hardheaded. Grandkids, you were probably born with those traits in your Kretoski DNA. You will need to be mindful of this, and then always try to be submissive to God and to stay faithful.

I had graduated from Ferris State University, and we were living in the old homestead house in Chippewa Lake. We had sold our mobile home and were now looking for a home to buy. We called realtors and kept reading the ads in the paper. Everything was too expensive or just very nasty and rundown. We just patiently kept looking. One day one of us noticed a nondescript ad in the *Big Rapids Pioneer*, the local newspaper. It read something like, "House for Sale: three-bedroom home, two-car garage, nine acres bordered by a trout stream." It was also in our price range and on a land contract. We talked with the seller and then looked at the property. The house wasn't great, but it was adequate. Your grandma and grandpa really wanted to buy this home. The only problem was that the seller wanted a $4,000 down payment, and we were pretty much broke. I could not find a job in my area of study after graduation, so I was working at a nursing home as an orderly. I just had to swallow my pride and work where I could find a job. It did not pay much, but I surely learned a lot in the five years that I worked there. We did not want to ask anyone for the money and went to the bank to try to borrow it. We found that we couldn't borrow money without collateral. Collateral is just a big word that means that if someone gives you a loan, you need to have something to give back, in case you can't make your payments. We had two cars that were not worth much and just a few personal belongings. We were denied a loan, and I was very frustrated. I was just looking at the waves like Peter had and was not being very patient. In my frustration I called a banker friend. He very kindly told me, "Sorry, Joe, but you have to have collateral." We wanted that house very badly. I stewed, fretted, and tried to work things out in my own way. There just had to be a way, but there really wasn't a way, humanly speaking. One evening while sitting in the living room talking to Grandma, I made a statement. I was tired, frustrated, and ready to throw in the towel. I said to her, "If God wants us to have this house, He is going to have to work out the circumstances." What do you think happened? I had finally given the situation to God. I was no longer hardheaded and working things out in my own power. I had finally become submissive to the will of God and had given it all to Him. As soon as that statement came out of my mouth, the phone rang, and someone offered us $4,000! God only wanted us to surrender to His will! We now sat in that living room crying and praising God. We were in a state of astonishment. God had done another amazing miracle in our lives. We moved into that house on January 1, 1979. It was snowy, cold, and nasty, but we did not complain. There was only praise in our hearts.

"'Lord, if it is you,' Peter replied, 'tell me to come to you on the water.' 'Come,' He said. Then Peter got down out of the boat, walked on the water and came toward Jesus. But when he saw the wind, he was afraid and, beginning to sink, cried out, 'Lord, save me!' Immediately Jesus reached out His hand and caught him. 'You of little faith,' he said, 'why did you doubt?'"

MATTHEW 14:28–31 (NIV)

Grandkids, when you are facing life, and it is rough, don't ever, ever give up or lose faith. Jesus will never let you down, and your phone may ring with great news. Keep the faith!

It's Just A Car

There were many times growing up when I learned valuable lessons from observing my parents. I was one of the most fortunate boys alive to have your great-grandparents to be my parents. They loved God, their family, their church, and people in general. They were very giving people. Were they perfect? Of course not, but they were the nicest and best people I ever met on this earth. Dad was even willing to share his treasured bluegill fillets with people.

Again, I am not going to mention names in this story. I will refer to the people just as our neighbors. Our neighbors were very needy in many areas of their lives. They had problems with their marriage, finances, kids, etc. The father had insane anger issues and drank plenty of beer. Once I watched him throw all the dishes that were in the sink out the kitchen window, because he was angry about something. Isn't it terrible how people cope with difficulties in life? The people they hurt the most are normally their own families. At any rate, Great-Grandpa wanted to help them and lead them to Jesus. I'm sure that he talked to them about Jesus. He talked to everyone about Jesus. That is just who he was. He took advantage of every opportunity to tell people about the God that changed his life and his legacy. Oftentimes, people don't care what you know until they know that you care. My mom and dad tried to help them in areas of need such as their need for a car. I think we still had our station wagon but also a '59 Ford. Great-Grandpa sold that neighbor that nice '59 Ford for only $200. Even as a young kid, I knew that was a terrific deal. The neighbors needed transportation, and we had an extra car. Don't ask me how I knew Dad sold the car for $200. I was just nosey and found things out! I watched this situation, wondering if the guy would actually pay Great-Grandpa. The neighbor never paid one single, solitary penny. I remember questioning my dad about the situation. I was upset with the guy. He very much took advantage of my dad. I wanted my dad to confront the man about the money, or at least take the car back. Dad's response was, "Joey, it's just a car. God always takes care of us." His response was simple yet so profound. This life is so much more than "things" and money. I thought the guy was a dirty rip-off, and he probably was. I would see that '59 Ford and have unpleasant thoughts enter my head about that guy, but Great-Grandpa just let it go. "It was just a car."

"Set your affection on things above, not on things on the earth."

COLOSSIANS 3:2 (KJV)

I am not conveying in this story that Christians should be pushovers and weak. Your great-grandfather was the strongest and most fearless person I ever met on this earth. He was also the most spiritual man I ever knew. He loved God with all of his heart, soul, and mind. I am not conveying that if we sell something, we should not expect to be paid. I am saying that our primary affection should be God and making Heaven our future home. Let's never allow "stuff" to become our main purpose in life and to distort our vision of eternity. I love my home and property. I sure like my boat and 9.9 Mercury motor. I am rather fond of my St. Croix fishing rods and my .243 deer rifle. Can these tangible things ever compare to family, love, relationships, and Heaven? Not even for a second. Grandkids, love life, and live it to its fullest, but always have Heaven, spiritual things, the church, and family as your primary love and focus. "Joey, it's just a car."

ICE

This next story is almost going to sound too bizarre to be true. I promise every word is factual and unembellished. This story took place while I was pastoring in Elkins, West Virginia. It was a small church that could only afford a small salary, and I mean a really small salary. I am not bemoaning this fact, but most people probably paid more in taxes than my yearly salary. It was a time when your grandma and I truly had to trust in God and His Word. Most people never have that privilege when they just have to believe the Scriptures and take God at His Word. Our car payment alone was almost as much as my monthly salary. We practically needed to pray for every bill and everything we needed. It was stressful at times but also a wonderful time of spiritual growth. God is so faithful.

While at Elkins, I "moonlighted" as a chimney sweep. Grandpa actually ended up on the front page of the local paper in his tuxedo and top hat while cleaning a chimney. My motto was "I can clean your chimney, but Jesus can clean your heart." That was stamped on the back of every business card. One day in March I received a phone call to come and clean a chimney. I should have had a clue about this job when it was a friend who made the phone call. The folks who needed their chimney cleaned lived so far out in the sticks that they had no phone. They used their CB to notify their friend to set up an appointment. I asked my good friend, Ray, to be my guide. What I did not realize is that they not only lived in the "sticks," but way, way out in the sticks. Ray took me on Route 33, and we traveled into the beautiful mountains. After driving for a while in my rather new Mercury Lynx station wagon, we turned left onto some dirt road. No, Grandkids, I did not have a four-wheel-drive truck. I do believe that Ray said this road would take us to the Red River. It was not just by the river, but into the river. This was not in the middle of the summer when the rivers were low, but in the springtime when they were normally at their highest. We stopped at the river and just looked at each other. I should have turned around immediately and headed back to Elkins. We both got out of my Lynx and walked to the river's edge. The water was moving swiftly and was higher than the bottom of my car doors. The river was approximately thirty-five feet wide at this crossing. I then made one of the dumbest and riskiest decisions of my entire life. I look back at this and just shake my head in bewilderment at my judgment. I decided to cross the trout stream. I backed up my trusty Lynx a short distance, put it in first, let out the clutch slowly, and pushed the accelerator. Somehow we hydroplaned it to the other side. God was good to us. We sat there on the other side almost shaking with excitement. We were filled with adrenaline. I looked at Ray and commented that we had to cross that crazy river again to get home. We kept driving those wild and winding mountainous roads. We were definitely in wild, wonderful West Virginia. The road finally led into a two-track. It was impassable for that little station wagon. Ray and I carried as many chimney brushes and rods as humanly possible and started walking up that two-track. We spotted the house in about a half mile or so. A mother and her teenage daughter lived there. The husband had died, but they remained in the house. The house was not log, but it was a rather rugged wood structure. These folks were literally mountain people who just wanted to live in this demanding environment. They told us many stories and showed us pictures of their pet bear cubs. They were very fascinating as they talked with their mountain colloquialisms. We eventually cleaned their chimney, had prayer with them, and left. They were rather poor, and I did not charge them. The lady was proud and wanted to pay. I told her that the stories and their hospitality were ample pay. When Ray and I arrived, it was sunny and above freezing. Remember these were mountain roads with the winter runoffs flowing across the road. When we left that late afternoon, it was still a beautiful, clear day, but the temperature had dropped drastically. We began to drive that narrow, winding road back to civilization. We were driving up a rather steep grade when suddenly the dependable little Lynx started sliding backward down that mountain road. We were sliding to the edge of the road and almost over the drop-off. Finally the car stopped sliding, but we were still stuck on ice. Yes, Grandkids, I was terrified, and my legs were shaking. Ray slowly got out of the car and crept to my side. All I could see were very big trees and the river way below in the bottom of that canyon. Ray would push the side of the car as I slowly let off the brake. With almost supernatural strength, Ray was able to push the car away from the cliff. I would release the brake a little, and the car would slide back toward the edge. Ray must have had a little traction from gravel and would try to push the car away from the cliff. I don't know how long it took, but we miraculously got off the ice, and I carefully backed to the bottom of the hill. Ray and I were both emotional wrecks. I thought I was going to slide over the cliff, and Ray thought the car was going to topple on him. It was actually very frightening, and we still had to cross that crazy river. We kept trying to navigate that steep hill. I would drive as close as I could to the mountain side of the road with Ray pushing the back bumper. We would hit that ice and start spinning and sliding. I would start sliding toward that cliff again, and Ray would try to push the car back toward the mountain. It was traumatic and so dreadfully nerve-racking. We did this driving and sliding several times. We were in desperate straits and only had one alternative. Yep, Grandkids, you guessed it. I got out of that car, and Ray and I prayed on that mountain road. I don't know how strong my faith was at that point, but two men were praying to God in desperation. What I did not mention is that Ray had only recently been saved. He got saved on the first Sunday in March, so he was only a baby Christian. We both got back into the car this time. I started driving up that steep incline, hit the ice, and never spun a tire. Ray said, "God had to be pushing the car!" We then drove up several steep hills and, even more dangerously, down some hills on those icy roads. We never slipped or spun a tire. God did a miracle and surely built the faith of a new Christian. When we approached the river, we never even slowed down. After driving on the icy roads, that river was a "piece of cake." It did not even cause any anxiety. God was pushing our car, and nothing could stop us now. I must admit that once we got back on Route 33, I was still an emotional wreck. My faith in God had grown amazingly, but my legs continued to shake uncontrollably.

As I look back on this experience, I think this was all God's providence and His plan. Ray became a man of faith, and as long as I knew him, he never doubted God.

"He giveth power to the faint; and to them that have no might He increaseth strength. Even the youths shall faint and be weary, and the young men shall utterly fall: But they that wait upon the LORD shall renew their strength; they shall mount up with wings as eagles; they shall run, and not be weary; and they shall walk, and not faint."

ISAIAH 40: 29–31 (KJV)

They can also drive on icy roads and cross raging rivers and not faint! We serve a great and wonderful God. Grandkids, God is able to deliver you from any type of situation. Never, ever give up—even when you think you might go over a cliff!

WASHING MACHINE

This is a story that occurred while we were pastoring in Elkins, West Virginia. We were rather poor financially but were so blessed in other areas. We really did not make our finances a focal point. There were too many other areas of concern. We also started a Christian school during our second year there and were very busy with ministry. When we had bills we needed to pay or essentials we could not afford, we earnestly prayed. Grandma and Grandpa learned that there were things we thought were important that really weren't. We stopped going out to eat for a long time. Eating out was nice but not essential. Don't think that we were unhappy people, because we were contented most of the time. Money is nice, and I would have never complained about having too much money, but money and possessions have never brought a person lasting contentment and satisfaction.

Joey was a baby at this time, and we used cloth diapers, not disposable diapers. Yes, we used those stinky cloth diapers that needed to be rinsed off and stuffed in a bucket until washed. It was disgusting but just a part of our lives and the lives of many others. Today most people are somewhat spoiled with all the conveniences that we have to make life easier. Grandkids, I am not being critical. I surely like my inside bathroom and many other things. It was during this time of nasty diapers when our washing machine began to malfunction. It would wash, but not transition into the rinse cycle, leaving soaking wet clothes and diapers.

Your unfortunate grandma had to manually wring everything out, and it was rough on her. What do you think we did? Yes, you're right again! We began to pray for a washing machine. Your grandma showed me the exact Kenmore washing machine she desired out of the Sears catalog. She liked it because it had an automatic fabric softener dispenser built into it. I literally prayed for that Kenmore washing machine. One day Grandma, Betsy, Joey, and I drove that trusty Lynx to Buckhannon to visit my aunt and uncle. We had never visited them since we had moved back to West Virginia. We got reacquainted and were chit-chatting when my uncle asked me a question: "Joey, do you need any appliances?" Have you ever been kind of embarrassed and hopeful at the same time? I did not want to scream out that we needed a washing machine, but I kind of mumbled that we needed a washing machine. He took me out to his garage, and what do you think was there? A refrigerator or stove? No! There sat the most gorgeous washing machine in the whole state of West Virginia— the exact Kenmore washing machine that Grandma had chosen from the Sears catalog. My uncle said, "You can have it if you want it." I was struggling to keep my emotions under control, but graciously and humbly accepted his offer. Grandma was very grateful and thrilled beyond words. My aunt and uncle owned a Sears store, and a lady bought that washing machine. It had one problem. The motor had a barely discernible weird noise in it that bothered her. They tried but could not repair it. My uncle had to take the washing machine back and could not sell it. It had been stuck in his garage for a few weeks, and he just did not know what to do with it. He knew it was brand new and in perfect condition. From his house to our house was approximately forty-five minutes. He brought it to our house and set it up. Grandma and Grandpa have been deeply appreciative of my aunt and uncle for many years.

We owned that washing machine for many years. It never lost that weird noise in the motor. It bothered that woman, but it was music to our ears. I thanked God many times as I heard that noise over the years. By the way, I was sure glad when Joey got potty-trained, and we got rid of those cloth diapers!

"Delight thyself also in the Lord: and He shall give thee the desires of thine heart."

PSALM 37:4 (KJV)

"But seek ye first the kingdom of God, and His righteousness; and all these things shall be added unto you."

MATTHEW 6:33 (KJV)

Always place your trust in God and not in riches. Jesus cares deeply about my grandkids. He even knows how many hairs are on your head. Take all your needs and burdens to Him. You have heard this many times from me, but don't ever, ever give up. Someday we will be in Heaven together as a family. What an amazing thought!

CHRISTMAS CELEBRATION

Here is another true story of God's kindness and care for his children. This story took place in Elkins, West Virginia, while I was pastoring there. It was just a few days before Christmas, and I was driving through Buckhannon. On a whim I decided to stop at the Sears store and visit with my aunt and uncle. They were very warm and pleasant to me. My uncle began giving me the "grand tour" of their store. It was rather intriguing as he explained different things about Buckhannon and their store. I still remember him discussing Craftsman tools. They came with a lifetime guarantee, and, of course, he would replace broken tools. The problem was that people would find discarded tools that he probably had thrown out at the dump and returned them the second time. He would need to honor the warranty. It became necessary for him to crush those Craftsman tools. He took me into the back storage area and described Sears' procedures. He also showed me the returned items and explained how they dealt with them. It was all new to me and very interesting.

Then he asked me a question. Remember, Grandkids, this is the same person who asked me if I needed any appliances. He asked me if there were any people in my church who needed Christmas gifts. As my emotions almost raced out of control, one more time I answered, "Yes." There were several families in the church that barely had money for gifts. I know that Christmas is about Jesus and not gifts, but on the other hand, wasn't Jesus the best Gift ever? You'd better believe He was, but it sure is nice to receive a gift or two on Christmas! My uncle, bless his heart, began to load my Lynx. These were items and gifts that people had returned to his store. At that time I owned a Mercury Lynx station wagon. I stood there in a total state of shock. He loaded toys, clothes, and all kinds of items into that car. He filled the whole back of the station wagon and kept bringing gifts out of the store. He then proceeded to fill the passenger seat with gifts. I could not believe what was happening. It was so surreal and utterly fantastic. Finally the loyal Lynx was completely loaded, and I tried to thank my aunt and uncle. Have you ever tried to express your gratitude when there were no words worthy to describe your thankfulness? I blubbered the best I could and drove out of Buckhannon with tears streaming down my face and my heart overflowing with praise to a kind and loving Heavenly Father. I rejoiced all the way back to Elkins. The only way this trip could have become better is if a bunch of reindeer would have appeared and got harnessed to the Lynx. (Grandpa sure has a crazy imagination, maybe because of old age or heart medicine!) I was definitely excited to get home and explain to Grandma what had occurred. She was rather excited herself. Then we unloaded every gift into our living room. Betsy and Joey were also excited as they began to understand the significance of what was happening. My heart was full of praise as we divvied up gifts for needy families. It was so much fun just putting a certain gift with a specific person, knowing that the gift would be deeply appreciated. Nobody in our church knew that Grandpa would be bringing them gifts. This was going to be a total surprise. As I drove from house to house and dropped off gifts, it was thrilling to see the reactions of the families. We had wrapped the gifts and put names on each package. These folks had little money for gifts and were receiving more gifts than they could have ever imagined. People were so thankful. They cried, sat in astonishment, and praised God. What a wonderful Savior Who had provided for them greatly during this time that we celebrate Jesus! There were also gifts for adults. Your grandma wore a coat that she received for many years.

This was definitely one of the most fulfilling Christmases I have ever experienced. It really is more blessed to give than to receive.

"For to us a child is born, to us a Son is given, and the government will be on His shoulders. And He will be called Wonderful Counselor, Mighty God, Everlasting Father, Prince of Peace."

ISAIAH 9:6 (NIV)

CHRISTMAS SURPRISE

Family has always been important to Grandpa and Grandma. It is special to get together during the holidays and other times during the year. I always enjoyed driving to Arthurdale, West Virginia, and walking into my mom and dad's home. We would smell freshly baked bread, pepperoni rolls, and pies. Oftentimes, there would be several different types of pies sitting on the washer and dryer as we walked in. The welcome was always special as we always felt accepted and loved. It was loud and crazy as we played games and reminisced. Great-Grandma would be scurrying around making sure everything was ready for the meal, and then was too antsy to really enjoy it very much. That's who she was—always serving and caring for others. Great-Grandpa was always tinkering with the woodstove. He would open the stove doors, and the smoke would pour out. He had to keep the home piping hot. Mom cooked traditional meals on certain holidays, but my favorite meal was fried bluegills. They were the best ever. I never grew tired of them, and every time I eat fish, I think of my parents. What great memories!

One time your great-grandparents were pastoring a church in St. Albans, West Virginia, and it was almost Christmas. All three of my sisters and their families were going to be there. Mom and Dad called and asked if we were going to be able to come. They were not too happy when I told them I could not get off work. It was actually the truth at the beginning until I worked out a schedule change with somebody. I would

71

need to work about ten straight days, and then I could get a few days off at Christmas. The great-grandparents would call, and we never updated them as to the change. Yes, we were slightly deceitful in a well-meaning way. Your grandma and grandpa were sneaking to West Virginia from Michigan just before Christmas. When we arrived in St. Albans, we needed to find the parsonage. We located it and drove by slowly. We then parked down the street, so we would not be seen. There was a houseful of people, and nobody knew we were coming. We sneaked up the sidewalk and went up the steps to the front door. We knocked on the door with great anticipation, looking forward to the surprise. Our expectations were fully met. Great-Grandma opened the door. She had the most surprised and incredulous look on her face and kept repeating, "I can't believe it, I can't believe it, I can't believe it." She was in tears as she hollered that Joey and Dawn were there. Then there was an avalanche of family who welcomed us warmly. What a great Christmas that was with family and what great memories! I am so blessed to have been born into a family that always loved and accepted me. I did fight with Vicki sometimes as we had to sleep with each other when we were little, but she shouldn't have kept coming on my side!

That was a wonderful Christmas reunion with no family missing. It is difficult now when we have family "get-togethers" with Great-Grandma and Great-Grandpa gone. They are now in Heaven. All who knew them have fond memories and continue to miss them. One thing we need to remember is that someday there will be the greatest reunion ever in Heaven. We surely don't want any family members missing at that great and last reunion. Can you imagine being together forever and forever in eternity? I am not totally confident this will happen, but can you imagine having a Kretoski fish fry with Jesus there? That's a wild thought, but we really don't know.

Grandkids, your great-grandpa would say, "There is a Hell to shun and a Heaven to gain." Don't allow anything to distract you from serving Christ and making Heaven your eternal home. Please don't miss that last reunion.

"No, dear brothers and sisters, I have not achieved it, but I focus on this one thing: Forgetting the past and looking forward to what lies ahead."

PHILIPPIANS 3:13 (NLT)

"He will wipe away every tear from their eyes, and death shall be no more, neither shall there be mourning, nor crying, nor pain anymore, for the former things have passed away."

REVELATION 21:4 (ESV)

Grandkids, you have never met your great-grandparents, but I hope and pray that someday you have that opportunity. I promise you that they can't wait to give you a hug that is out of this world.

BETTY'S DREAM

Betty is Grandpa's sister. She is an awfully special lady whom I genuinely respect. She seems shy and maybe a little introverted, especially around people she does not know. Betty would be very embarrassed that I wrote this, but she has been an inspiration to me for many years. She has suffered from rheumatoid arthritis since her early twenties and just won't give up. She forces herself to do things and won't quit. She even played on a softball team while suffering from rheumatoid arthritis. That is one determined woman! My respect for her has grown the last few years, when I found it necessary myself to deal with chronic pain. Chronic pain can really "mess" with you—body, soul, and spirit. Betty has dealt with it for fifty years and has somehow kept her head up. I'm thankful for her inspiration to her little brother and many others.

This story is about a dream that Betty had and that turned into much more than a dream. July 6, 2017, was a very significant day. That was the day when our youngest grandchild, Selah Joy, was born and also the day when Betty had her dream. The dream began with Betty looking up into a beautiful sky. She said that the colors were very brilliant and that she was seeing colors she had never even seen before. This was rather peculiar for Betty, because she had never dreamed in color before. It had always been black and white. This dream was in vivid colors. Grandkids, fasten your seatbelts, because this dream gets really good and exciting. This beautiful sky suddenly opened up, and many angels began to float down. It was during this angelic time that she heard a male voice giving a proclamation, "He's coming!" Betty knew this declaration was talking about Jesus. The Bible very powerfully teaches about Jesus returning, and Betty had just had this male voice reaffirm this Scriptural concept in a dream. Grandkids, I told you this was an exciting dream, and it only got better. Now remember that Betty was still dreaming. In her dream she said, "If He's coming, I had better start praying." This was exactly what she did in the dream. Betty prayed and cried, and then prayed and cried some more. It was at this point in her dream when she literally woke up. She was in real time then. Betty was no longer dreaming, but she continued to pray and cry. Betty was afraid she'd wake up her husband, George, so she got out of bed and walked to the living room. She sat on the couch and continued to pray and cry. She did not know how long she prayed and cried, but she was sure that God heard her prayer and saw her tears. God reached down and touched her heart and spirit. Betty continued to pray and cry but also began to laugh while thanking God for His "wonderful" touch. George woke up and came into the living room. He questioned Betty, "Babe, what's wrong?" Betty could only shake her head and then told George, "I have been touched by God, and it has been so long." George patted her on the leg and went outside. Betty just kept praying and thanking God, and she received "showers of blessings." I believe what she meant was that God kept continuously touching her heart. Our dad had a similar experience, but he described it as wave after wave of God's Spirit touching his heart. Betty said, "I thank Him every day for His touch and pray I will never forget. It has changed my life. Thank you, God!"

Grandkids, that is a humdinger of a testimony from Aunt Betty. I doubt there is even a small chance that she will ever forget this touching experience. Her testimony has touched my heart many times. I gave her testimony on the first night of camp meeting last summer and had many people thank me for sharing it, saying that it encouraged them greatly. I must also mention that if God touches you, you will be changed. That is a wild thought, but it is truth. When a person is born again or saved, then God literally lives inside of them. This sounds too good to be true, but it's a fact. That is why people who are truly saved have strength to obey God and do His will. He gives us the power to make the right choices. We don't have to continue to live in willful sin. It is not our strength but God's strength. Only when God lives in us do we have the power to live right. God gives us the power of choice, and when we make right choices, He empowers us to complete what He has set before us. Religion is saturated with emotionalism and intellectualism, but the most important thing ever is when a person has a relationship with Jesus and continues to walk with Him day by day. That only happens if you have been touched by God, and God's Spirit resides in your body. That all seems so fantastic, but that is the key for a fulfilling life on this earth.

> "But if the Spirit of him that raised up Jesus from the dead dwell in you, He that raised up Christ from the dead shall also quicken your mortal bodies by His Spirit that dwelleth in you."
>
> ROMANS 8:11 (KJV)

GREAT-GRANDPA FORGIVES

This next story will probably be the most difficult story Grandpa has ever written. This is a true story that my father, your great-grandfather, told me. He found it very difficult to discuss his life growing up and his experiences during World War Two. One day while just the two of us were sitting in the living room, he began to talk to me about some of his experiences growing up and then as an adult. It was challenging and emotional as he shared some rather negative experiences with me, but the story ended with God's grace and healing. I struggled mightily with my emotions the day that my dad communicated about his life, and even today I became very emotional while trying to write this story. I have tried to relate this story while counseling people and find it so difficult. Grandkids, this is a wonderful story of forgiveness, and that is why I am sharing it with you. It just can't be forgotten, even though it is hard to talk about. There are some facts that I will purposefully leave out and other specifics I will not discuss in detail. Hopefully, you will get a pretty good idea what I am trying to convey surrounding this story and will especially understand the forgiveness aspect.

I want everyone who reads this story to realize that my father shared this story with sadness and a great sense of humility. He wishes that it had never happened, but it did. He never lost his thankful spirit to the true, living, and forgiving God.

Circumstances were awfully rough when Great-Grandpa's father passed away. I think Great-Grandpa was only nine years old, and there were six children altogether—four girls and two boys. Great-Grandpa was the oldest son. He told me how he tried to support the family even as a youngster by sometimes fishing for catfish most of the night and then selling them. He would also knock coal off the trains, collect the coal in bags, and then sell it. Yes, he knew it was stealing, but he was trying to help the family to survive. He told me he had jars of illegal liquor hidden all over those hillsides in West Virginia and which he sold. They kept a bathtub half filled with water in case the police decided to search their house. They would pour the liquor into the tub of water to dilute it. Great-Grandpa told me it was a miracle of God that he never got bitten by a copperhead as he trekked over those hillsides. The Kretoski family was very poor and was just trying to survive. It was during these desperate times when Great-Great-Grandma Kretoski got married to a local Russian coal miner. There were three more children—two boys and a girl—born into the already large family.

Grandkids, now is the time in this story when I am choosing to become rather vague and ambiguous. I don't ever want to embarrass or hurt family members who are still living. Let's just say that there were some very tough situations that were encountered by the children and Great-Great-Grandma. People were mistreated at times. My dad carried this hurt and anger into his adulthood and allowed a root of bitterness to live in his heart. There were things that happened for which he was unwilling to forgive his stepfather. The next section of this story is very sensitive, so I will try to continue carefully. Your great-grandpa and his stepfather were drinking at a local bar. Remember this occurred before Great-Grandpa was saved. The stepfather called Great-Great-Grandma a bad name, and all that pent-up anger, hurt, and bitterness exploded in Great-Grandpa's heart. He lost control of himself and began beating his own stepfather. It was extremely difficult and emotional for both of us as my dad continued with the story. In his words he said, "I just remember hitting him time after time after time." Finally some men pulled Great-Grandpa off his stepfather and told him, "Joe, you have to stop. You are going to kill him." I don't remember precisely what happened after the beating, but Dad told me that his stepfather was very much afraid of him after that. When he visited his mother, his stepfather would sneak out the back door and leave in fear. This went on for some time. I don't recall the time that had transpired between the beating and August 6, 1956. That day changed everything. That is the day when Great-Grandpa was saved and received forgiveness. There was a drastic change in his behavior, but his heart and mind were also changed. My dad told me the next time he saw his stepfather leave the house in fear, he chased him down. He told me that he cowered in fear. He thought he was going to receive another beating. Great-Grandpa told me that he said, "George, you never have to fear me again. I have been saved, and I forgive you!" God had miraculously changed Great-Grandpa's actions and attitudes when he got saved. When God truly comes to reside in a person, that person is changed.

I realize that for many people who have been hurt, forgiveness takes time and is a process. They may even need guidance from a trained Christian therapist to work through different areas of abuse. For your great-grandpa, forgiveness of others was instantaneous. Does this imply that Great-Grandpa never struggled with his past memories of World War Two or his mistreatment? Though he loved God more than any person I ever knew, he still struggled with nightmares as an elderly man. I heard moaning and groaning with my own ears as he slept. It surely made me think as my mom and I discussed this situation. We need to have a lot of compassion and empathy for people as they deal with their past. With God's help people can get "past their past"!

"And we know that all things work together for good to those who love God, to those who are called according to His purpose."
ROMANS 8:28 (NKJV)

"Get rid of all bitterness, rage and anger, brawling and slander, along with every form of malice. Be kind and compassionate to one another, forgiving each other, just as in Christ God forgave you."

EPHESIANS 4:31–32 (NIV)

I used this quotation one other time in this book but would like to use it again. Corrie ten Boom said, "Forgiveness is to set a prisoner free, and to realize the prisoner was you." Grandkids, you will be hurt by others. That is part of life. Never allow bitterness to creep into your heart. Always forgive!

OUT OF DARKNESS AND INTO MARVELOUS LIGHT

This next story is the best and most important story that was ever written about the Kretoskis. It is the story of how the Lord saved Great-Grandpa, and his life and heart were transformed. This is what changed the legacy of our family. This story was not written by Grandpa, but by your great-grandpa Kretoski. It is written verbatim off a tract that Great-Grandpa had published, although there are a few editing changes. This is the beginning of when the Kretoski family was radically changed.

"On August 8, 1956, about midnight, my whole life was instantly changed by the revelation I had of Jesus Christ through the power of His Holy Spirit. Oh! The joy, peace, comfort, and assurance that was mine from sins forgiven. This is the greatest blessing a person can enjoy this side of heaven.

"The following is my testimony of grace: how the Lord so graciously convicted me of sin, righteousness, and judgment to come; how He saved me, sanctified me, and then called me to preach this glorious gospel.

"The changed life of a neighbor caused me to start thinking on eternal things. I was walking by the ballpark near our home when I noticed our neighbor with a group of small boys, managing the ball team. He was playing a recorder, and the music was hymns. I was astonished at his kind way of speaking to the boys. This did not sound like the neighbor I had gambled and drunk with so many times. I was so impressed with his changed life that I went immediately home and told my wife about it. She went over and asked his wife what had happened to him. She came back telling me that our neighbor had been saved. Saved? Saved from what? Her reply was, 'How should I know?'

"Sometime later my wife attended a prayer meeting in a little Methodist church in my hometown. When she came home and told me how everyone asked for prayer for their children and then told what God was doing for them, I told her not to go back there anymore; those people were crazy. After all, I belonged to the Catholic Church where I had been taught that only Catholics would go to heaven.

"Once again my wife attended prayer meeting, and this time she told me how she acted. She began crying right in the meeting. The preacher came to her and asked if she wanted to be saved, and she told him, 'No.' The people of the church did not realize how ignorant we were of the Scriptures and real salvation. I am so thankful for the woman from that church who came to our home to see my wife. I was in bed in the next room when I heard voices in the kitchen. The lady was telling my wife, 'You can be saved and know it.' Here was that word 'saved' again. My wife told the lady she did not know if she believed that or not, but the lady told her how God had saved her and about her husband being saved. She really told of God's grace. When the woman left, I ran out of the bedroom and told my wife that this woman was crazy, or I was all mixed up. I found out later that I was all mixed up. This was the first testimony of saving grace that I had ever heard. At the age of thirty-one, I had spent six years in the U.S. Navy and been around the world, but no one had ever talked to me about my soul.

"One afternoon as I was getting ready for work, my wife said, 'Joe, let me read something to you.' She read the New Testament to me for the first time in my life. (To this day we do not know how the New Testament came into our home.) Every morning she would read this Book to me, and every night when I came home from work, she would read to me, and we would try to understand what we read.

"It was during this time that conviction settled down on my heart. I could not understand what this guilty feeling was, what this awful, condemning feeling was. I only knew that inside of me something was happening.

"About three months had gone by since I heard about my neighbor getting saved and several weeks since my wife started reading the New Testament to me, and deep conviction was inside me.

"I quit smoking. As I started to work one afternoon, I lit up a cigarette, threw the rest of the pack to my wife, and told her she would never see me smoke again. She laughed, because she had heard me say this many times before. I had started smoking when I was eight years old, but that was the last time. There was a voice deep within me saying it was wrong. I can remember the last time I ever got drunk.

"I was a very selfish person and would lie, cheat, or do whatever I had to do to get my way. Under conviction I quit lying. I never went to church, but, oh, the power that was in that New Testament being read to me each day. I even made restitutions during this time.

"I can remember my last day as a sinner. It was the most miserable day of my life. I was a welder, and each time I put my welder's helmet down, I would have to jerk it up, because all I could think about was God. I just could not work. I was thankful when the shift was completed.

"When the day was over and the children in bed, my wife again was reading the Word to me. She was reading the third chapter of John and the questions that Nicodemus was asking Jesus. How can a man be born again? What does this mean? Neither of us knew. My last words as a sinner were, 'If we are ever going to be saved, we are going to have to do something about it.' Immediately something happened to me. I found myself on my knees beside the bed, saying, 'Oh, my God! Oh, my God!' He was my God now, and He was flooding my soul with His grace. I did not say one 'Hail Mary' or one 'Our Father,' but wave after wave of glory came into my heart. I knew I was saved. All the condemnation was gone. I was free! My sins were forgiven, and I knew Jesus Christ in reality. This was the end of all the confusion; the burden was lifted. I was so happy that I wanted the whole world to know about my newfound joy."

Wow, Grandkids, that was exciting! Your great-grandpa never went to bed that night. He praised God all night. Great-Grandma Kretoski continued to search for God for six months. She needed to process her own "self-righteousness." She was good and wholesome, especially when she compared herself to Dad, but still needed Jesus. Her "saving experience" was not as dramatic as Great-Grandpa's, but it was just as real. God also saved her and lived in her heart.

Grandkids, you might ask the question, "Can a person really change immediately after getting saved?" If the person is truly saved and the Spirit of God has entered his heart, there will be a true change. There is no doubt about it.

"But you are a chosen people, a royal priesthood, a holy nation, God's special possession, that you may declare the praises of Him who called you out of darkness into His wonderful light."

1 PETER 2:9 (NIV)

Jesus says, "Very truly I tell you, no one can see the kingdom of God unless they are born again."

JOHN 3:3 (NIV)

Massasauga

Here goes another snake story. This story took place in Michigan when Great-Grandpa was pastoring in Jackson. We moved to Jackson during the summer of 1967. I was going into seventh grade and would attend an inner-city school. This was a good experience for me, because I had never associated much with black kids or other ethnic groups. Now I was one of the only few "white boys" who were on the football team. Talking about football, this was the time when I played against Tony Dungy. Yes, that is the same guy who coached Tampa Bay to a Super Bowl win. I never beat him, either! We were opposing quarterbacks. Some of my best friends in school were African Americans. I learned a lot about tolerance and love when your great-grandpa would preach at a local black church. He and that black pastor became good friends. That was rather significant because it was a time of racial unrest. I remember sitting on the curb of Michigan Avenue in Jackson and watching the riot fires. Your great-grandma became anxious about me being out during this time and came looking for me. I was returning to the parsonage when she stepped out from the edge of the church. She still had on her long, flowing nightgown. She scared me half out of my wits! There was much tension and violence at school. It got really crazy the day when Martin Luther King was assassinated. There was so much screaming and threatening in the hallways. Several students were beat up in the hallways and outside the school. School was dismissed early that day. It was such a time of upheaval and turmoil. I'm so thankful that Jesus is not a racist and that he died for everyone. Even though we may have had some racism in our family, even one member in the Ku Klux Klan, it does not mean that we can't love everybody. I used to tell the guys at Pineview that I was color blind. I am thankful for those two years in Jackson.

Now I need to get back to my story. A massasauga is a rattlesnake that lives in the southern part of Michigan. It normally lives in swampy areas. Great-Grandpa, Grandpa, and Maynard were fishing on Lime Lake. We did not have a motor so you know exactly who was rowing: Grandpa! I really did not mind rowing. It was like lifting weights and would only make me stronger. I was sitting in the middle seat. The two men were fishing for bluegill, and I was fishing for bass. We saw a moving ripple in the water and thought it was a water snake. We just kept fishing and did not get too worried over a water snake. Somehow this snake slithered up the side of the boat and reared its triangular head. Yes, it was another rattlesnake, and it was only about a foot away from me! Great-Grandpa and Maynard reacted quickly, and each grabbed an oar. I sat there terrified and ready to dive out of the boat—literally! I can still see that head swaying back and forth and those slitty eyes. Why that rattlesnake did not crawl into the boat, I don't know, but I am sure grateful it didn't. It slipped back into the lake. I know it is not "politically correct" to kill snakes these days, but your great-grandpa whacked that snake with his oar, and I snagged it with my fishing pole. The two men weren't too happy that I snagged it, but we rowed to shore and killed it.

There will be times in life when bad things will happen or rough circumstances will raise their ugly heads. Many people will want to jump out of the boat or run away. Sometimes we just need to be steady and wait. Trust God, and trust your friends. Great-Grandpa and Maynard grabbed the oars, and I sat there helplessly, but they were ready to protect me. True friends will always have your "back!" Life is good most of the time, but difficult times will come. It is hard to understand why bad things happen to good people. We do know that the rain will fall on the just and the unjust.

"Finally, my brethren, be strong in the Lord, and in the power of His might. Put on the whole armour of God, that ye may be able to stand against the wiles of the devil. For we wrestle not against flesh and blood, but against principalities, against powers, against the rulers of the darkness of this world, against spiritual wickedness in high places. Wherefore take unto you the whole armour of God, that ye may be able to withstand in the evil day, and having done all, to stand."

EPHESIAN 6:10–13 (KJV)

Grandkids, what a powerful and supportive Scripture this is! Remember, if you are truly saved, God lives inside of you. He will give you power to overcome if you don't allow your fears and anxieties to overwhelm you. Don't run, unless God wants you to run. Be strong and courageous in the Lord. Don't ever give up! Put on that armor!

Did You Pray, Too?

This is a story about chimney sweeping. I did "moonlight" as a chimney sweep in Michigan and West Virginia for a few years. This was the only time when Great-Grandpa ever went with me. I never really knew what I was getting into until I arrived. I knew I would be in trouble cleaning this chimney by looking at the roof. It was an old two-story farmhouse with the steepest roof I had ever seen. Normally I would put a ladder up and just carefully walk to the chimney. This roof was too treacherous. I carried a 100-foot rope in my vehicle just for situations like this. I extended the ladder, climbed to the edge of the roof, and tossed the rope over the roof. Of course, I held on to one end of the rope. I climbed back down the ladder and tied the end of the rope, I think, to a tree. I then climbed back up the ladder with my equipment and tied the rope around my waist. I then cautiously pulled myself to the peak of the roof. Yes, Grandkids, I was nervous and asking God for assistance. I was also hoping I tied a good knot to that tree. I had to totally trust that rope. Finally, I straddled the peak of the roof and carefully walked to the chimney. The chimney was almost completely plugged with creosote. I used the smallest brush that I had and tried to brush out a bigger opening. The original size was eight inches by twelve inches. I pushed the small brush into the chimney and proceeded to get it stuck. I mean really stuck. I could not move it an inch. I was rather strong back then, but I could not budge the brush. I was leaning against that chimney, and I pulled up on the rods as hard as I possibly could. The brush did not move, but that chimney actually swayed away from the house a short distance. I thought the whole chimney was going to crumble with me on it. Somehow, someway, that chimney came back to its original position. Thank you, Jesus! I was in a horrible predicament and trying not to have a panic attack. I was sweating, breathing crazily, and my heart was trying to pound out of my chest. I attempted to calm myself and did the only thing I knew to do. I bowed my head up on that two-story house, and prayed that God would loosen that brush. I tried not to lean on the chimney and, with a little leverage, pulled up on those rods. To my great relief, that brush moved easily. Your great-grandpa looked up to me and asked, "Did you pray, too?" God had miraculously loosened the brush, and I cleaned that chimney with no more complications. I am also thankful the knot held as I gingerly climbed off that steep roof.

God has helped and protected me so many times. This story is just one more example of God's care.

"God is our refuge and strength, a very present help in trouble."

PSALM 46:1 (KJV)

"Behold, I am the Lord, the God of all flesh. Is anything too hard for me?"

JEREMIAH 32:27 (ESV)

Grandkids, it is so easy to become dependent upon all our gadgets, technology, and all of our current conveniences. There are times we forget that there is a God who does supernatural acts. He is our haven and protector. Don't ever lose sight or faith in this magnificent God.

I Can't Swim!

This is another Shenandoah River story. I have grown to love the Muskegon River in Michigan, but the Shenandoah River was special to me growing up in West Virginia. I have so many fond memories of that river: catching smallmouth bass and channel cats, those important talks with my dad, tubing, sitting around the campfire, pumping up the lantern, and eating salami sandwiches and boiled eggs. When your great-grandpa and I went fishing, we did not cook much. Normally we ate cereal for breakfast. I remember fishing and camping with Joey and eating like kings. We would have Grandma's goulash the first evening. We would have fried fish, grilled chicken, and grilled sausage. For breakfast we would have scrambled eggs, bacon, French toast, or pancakes. Anyway, Great-Grandpa and I slept in a tent, and he would be up fishing at daybreak. He never woke me up when we were camping. I remember sitting at camp in the morning, eating my cereal with lots of sugar, and here would come Dad walking down the tracks with a large stick over his shoulder loaded with two or three stringers filled with catfish and small-mouth. Guess what, Grandkids? I did not go fishing after that breakfast. I helped my dad clean fish. We did not fillet our fish back then. We would scale and gut the bass but would skin the cats with pliers. Skinning catfish was a hard job, and usually there were lots to clean. Great memories!

I was a pastor in Elkins, West Virginia, when this story happened. I took Great-Grandpa, a few guys from the church, and one guy from the community to the Shenandoah River. It was probably a two-and-a-half to a three-hour trip from Elkins. I was very excited. This was my first trip back to my cherished Shenandoah since we had moved to Michigan when I was twelve. We set up camp and went fishing. I tried to give the guys pointers and showed them where to fish. Great-Grandpa and I could not wait to get into the water. The others were very hesitant to wade. They were used to the trout streams surrounding Elkins where they would wear hip waders. I remember finally talking Ray into wading the river with me. He was very anxious, and I kept encouraging him. I am sure I laughed at him a few times, also. We would actually intertwine our arms together when we crossed a swifter and deeper spot. We caught several fish and returned to camp safely. The guys thought that I had lost my mind the next morning when I tubed across a rather dangerous spot. It was a big wide hole with a small waterfall below it. It looked like excellent fishing a couple hundred yards across the large hole. I lay on my belly, put my pole in my mouth, and paddled with my arms like a wild man. I did not want to get swept over the falls. I actually caught lots of fish that morning. I had a channel cat poke a hole in my tube and lost the use of it. They have very sharp side fins. By the way, I still have teeth marks in that pole to this day!

David wanted to go out wading with me the next day. He, too, was very nervous, so I just went very slowly and did the "arm clasp" through the more treacherous water. The river was approximately four hundred yards wide where we were wading. We usually fished near the middle of the river. Then I got this crazy idea about maybe wading to the far side and fishing downstream. That's what David and I did. We fished downstream for three or four hundred yards. We did not want to backtrack. It's a lot of hard work wading upstream, so we decided to try to cross over at the bottom of some rapids. These were the same rapids that I got stuck in when I was young and where my dad rescued me. We were now at the end of this long set of rapids, which flowed into a long and deep hole. I was rather uncertain myself about crossing this area. I never crossed here as a kid, and this was unknown territory. I did not think the water was over our heads, but it was swift and powerful. We each intertwined an arm and began our side shuffle across. I have not mentioned this, but David wasn't a small man. He was probably close to six feet tall and 250 pounds. We began to wade across slowly and cautiously. The water got deeper and deeper and was very powerful. In the beginning the water pounded our knees, and then we were up to our waists. We were not even halfway yet. We hung on to each other's arms in a "death grip." We just kept trying to slide our feet on the bottom of the river and hang on. We had one major problem. The river got deeper as we came to the middle of the crossing. The river was now hitting us in our chests powerfully, and we were having great difficulty keeping our feet down. We began to struggle mightily to stay upright while still clasping each other's arms. Our feet were swept out from under us suddenly, and I yelled desperately, "God, help us!" Grandkids, there is no exaggeration here. This is exactly what happened. Our feet immediately hit the bottom of the river, and we walked steadily without slipping or struggling and safely waded out of that treacherous current. Then David, who was not a Christian at that time, said, "I will always believe there is a God now. I can't even swim!" He "scared me to death" and thrilled me at the same time. I would have never even taken him into the river or definitely not even considered crossing at the bottom of the rapids. Thank God He did another miracle! There is no way that I could have rescued David if we had been swept into that deep hole. I would have never taken that risk. God took my ignorance and showed His power and care to David. As we made it back to the camp, David continued to express his gratitude to a living Heavenly Father. One more time God heard my prayer of desperation!

That was one exciting time! As I wrote this story, I relived many of those old emotions that I felt. Grandpa is deeply appreciative of God answering prayer instantly and of His great mercy.

Jesus said, "Indeed, the very hairs of your head are all numbered. Don't be afraid; you are worth more than many sparrows."

LUKE 12:7 (NIV)

Yes, Grandkids, you are very valuable to God. Is it any wonder that He sent His Son to this earth to teach, to die on the cross, and then to rise from the grave? And never forget that someday Jesus is coming back again. Don't be so distracted by earthly things that you allow your mind to be clouded about God and Heaven.

GOD'S EVERLASTING MERCY

This story took place in a nursing home. I began working there soon after I graduated from college. There just weren't many jobs available, and I took what was available. Sometimes we just need to walk through doors that God opens. Did I want to work in a nursing home as an orderly? Not even for a second. But as I sit here typing this story, I realize that God had a plan for my life and that working in a nursing home for about five years was part of that plan. God was molding me into the person He wanted me to become. Also, I was rather prideful, and working in a nursing home gave me a good dose of humility. God always knows what is best for us. We just need to be willing to be led and stay surrendered to God. It was also during those five years when God helped me to lead several elderly people to Jesus. This story is about one of those people.

When I hired in at the nursing home, the staff really had a difficult time with two ladies. The one was named Lillian, and nobody had anything nice to say about her. She was mean, stubborn, and uncooperative. Anytime I worked on the hallway where Lillian resided, the charge nurse put her in my care. I was always kind and respectful to her. I tried to cheer her up. Guess what, Grandkids? Lillian and I began to develop a really positive relationship. She would smile when I walked into her room and was so nice to me. The nursing home staff were all rather shocked at the change in Lillian. I began to take my breaks with Lillian, and we would just talk about "old times." We grew close to each other, and there was a special bond between us. I need to do the "Paul Harvey" thing and give you the "rest of the story." Lillian was Grandma's step-grandma. She had married Grandma's grandpa after Grandma's biological grandmother passed away. As I drew closer to Lillian, I began carefully to talk to her about Jesus. She was very old and had never been saved. I would ask her if she wanted me to pray with her or if she wanted to seek forgiveness. She would get a slightly perturbed look on her face and go into her stubborn mode. I just kept spending time with her, and many times your grandma would visit with her also. We did not give up. We kept praying and fasting that she would surrender to Jesus. Grandma and I knew that she was probably going to die soon. She was ninety-one years old, and her health was declining. We went to visit her one day, and she was so close to dying. She could not communicate in any way. We talked and prayed for her, and left the facility. We knew she was dying. Your grandma and I were pretty worried that Grandma Lillian would die without Jesus. We prayed and fasted for three days. We asked God to help us to communicate with Lillian and give us one more chance. We went back to visit Lillian in three days with rather burdened hearts. We knew that this was probably going to be our last chance to lead her to Jesus. Lillian could not talk but would follow us with her eyes and could move her head. After a minute or two, I asked Lillian the most important question that a person can ever ask another person: "Don't you want to accept Jesus into your heart?" She could not speak, but she spoke volumes when she nodded her head "yes!" At that moment she surrendered herself to Jesus and found forgiveness. Lillian was saved! God had extended His mercy and answered our prayers. Grandma and I were so very thankful and praiseful. Lillian would spend eternity in Heaven. Grandma Lillian passed away three days later and went to be with Jesus.

Wow! That is one of the most awesome stories ever. It is very rare that a person who is that elderly gives her heart to God. God is an amazing God. Though working in a nursing home would not have been my first choice for a job, it was God's plan. Remember that God will use you wherever He places you. Grandkids, may your heart always be surrendered and malleable toward God. His way is always the best way. Also remember that this life does not end it all. Do your best to lead people to Jesus.

"But because of His great love for us, God, who is rich in mercy, made us alive with Christ even when we were dead in transgressions—it is by grace you have been saved."

EPHESIANS 2:4–5 (NIV)

"The Lord is compassionate and gracious, slow to anger, abounding in love."

PSALM 103:8 (NIV)

Jesus said, "Follow me, and I will make you fishers of men."

MATTHEW 4:19 (KJV)

SKUNK

This next story is really essential but may sound a bit "preachy." Grandpa does have a tendency to be "preachy," but I know that someday I will be gone, and there are so many experiences and concepts that I don't want to be lost. That is the main reason I wrote *Grandpa's Stories*. When I pass on to eternity, I don't want these God stories to pass with me. There are stories that I have written that Grandma, your parents, and my sisters were not aware. Grandkids, just sit back and relax, but listen really well as I write about the skunk.

We had a dog that was mostly springer spaniel. He was a house dog, and you know what that means. Sometimes we had to get up in the middle of the night to let the dog out. Smokey was telling us he had to go potty, so I got out of bed, put my robe on, and took him out. Smokey was doing his doggy thing when I noticed movement near the garage. I went into panic mode when I realized that it was a skunk. I was screaming for Smokey to come to me, but as they say, "curiosity killed the cat." This time curiosity caused the "polecat" to lift its tail and let its rancid, nasty, putrid fluid fly. I could actually see the spray as it was projected in Smokey's direction. The skunk "high-tailed it" out of there, and Smokey suddenly became obedient. The crazy dog would have never gotten sprayed if he had listened to me the first time. Wow, that brings up an important point! Grandkids, you need to listen to your parents the first time, even if you don't understand. Put obedience first, and questions second. This will help you when you are older to follow the Bible and God's voice. Anyway, I did not allow Smokey back into the house. He went into the dog pen. I could not smell spray on my robe but left it outside on the porch just in case a smidgen of that noxious, disgusting spray had gotten on it. I quietly sneaked into the bedroom and then into the bed. I did not want to wake up Grandma. Grandma suddenly screeched like a wild banshee, "Get out of bed! You smell like a skunk!" I quickly got out of bed and was followed by Grandma. She told me I smelled horrible. I told her that I could not smell anything. I got my first bath in tomato juice and tried to get that lovely aroma scrubbed off my body. I slept on the couch the remainder of the night.

You're probably wondering where in the world I'm going with this story. This is it in a nutshell. Satan has a plan to destroy our relationship with Jesus or to have us grow cold in our relationship so that we are ineffective for the cause of Christ. Sometimes if Satan can get us to live close to the edge of sin or to the world, we begin to look like the world and smell like the world and be totally ignorant to this fact. Satan knows that we are probably not going to get wild and crazy, but if he can slowly get us to live a little closer to sin and cloud our minds, he will eventually destroy us spiritually. Oftentimes, we don't even know what has happened until it is too late. It's kind of like the live frogs placed into a pot of water. The water begins to heat up and then boil. Then before they realize it they are cooked and become frog legs. Sometimes people become so captivated by their church and its beliefs that Jesus is no longer their main focus. Anytime Jesus is not the main focus, the tendency is to grow cold spiritually. The process of backsliding has begun and will continue unless we come to our senses. This is just one of Satan's plans to destroy us. It happens, and we don't even know it.

If you live close to Jesus and walk daily with Him, this may never be an issue in your life, but many people have struggled in this area. I have actually seen people give up their faith and stop living for Jesus. It is tragic. Grandkids, always listen to God's voice, live by the Bible, and never ever give up. We all want to be at the great and last reunion in Heaven.

"Do not love the world or anything in the world. If anyone loves the world, love for the Father is not in them. For everything in the world—the lust of the flesh, the lust of the eyes, and the pride of life—comes not from the Father but from the world. The world and its desires pass away, but whoever does the will of God lives forever."

1 JOHN 2:15–17 (NIV)

Happy Hour

This story took place at the nursing home where I worked for about five years. After I had worked there for a few years, a new organization and family became owners. The new administrator and I became rather good friends. Your grandma and I even had them over for a meal. It was during this time that I was offered a new position, and I became the Director of Activities. The new job had plenty of perks, and I enjoyed it. It was wonderful to have every weekend off and to make my own schedule. There were times I would take Betsy to work with me, and the elderly folks always responded positively to her. She was a sweet little girl with flowing blond hair and a beautiful little smile.

The new job was great until I was confronted with one major issue—Happy Hour. The facility set up a "Happy Hour" once or twice a week, and I was supposed to be in charge. Grandkids, Happy Hour was a time when they would bring many of the residents to the dining room in the afternoon and serve them alcohol. Not only was I supposed to organize it, but I was to serve the alcohol. I struggled mightily with my conscience and whether I could really please God by doing this. This activity went totally against my value system. A value is something that we hold as important. There are certain things that we learn from our parents, and others that we learn from the Scriptures: a set of beliefs that we value and try to live by. I discussed the situation with the administrator, and he was sympathetic but still emphasized that it was part of my job responsibilities. I prayed and fasted, and tried to find an answer. I tried to rationalize and make excuses why it was okay to do it but knew deep in my heart that it was wrong. I knew that I could not please God by leading Happy Hour and serving alcohol. I wish I could say that this was an easy decision for me, but it wasn't. I had a bigger salary, great hours, good benefits, and the prestige of being a department head. It would have been better for me not to have taken the new position in the first place. I would be embarrassed, and people would really not understand.

Grandkids, there will come times in your life when you have to make decisions based on your values and whether you are going to please God. As difficult as it was for me, I had to quit being the activities director and went back to being an orderly. Almost everyone thought that I had lost my mind. I was questioned repeatedly for days. I did my best to explain why and tried to move on. My conscience was clear, and to this day I feel strongly that I made the right decision. Was it easy? No! Was it right? Yes!

"Am I now trying to win the approval of human beings, or of God? Or am I trying to please people? If I were still trying to please people, I would not be a servant of Christ."

GALATIANS 1:10 (NIV)

"But Peter and the apostles answered, 'We must obey God rather than men.'"

ACTS 5:29 (ESV)

Always listen to God's voice and obey the Bible.

Pride Goes Before
Destruction

Grandkids, you know how I love to float the river and fish for small-mouth bass. On this particular float I was fishing with Gary. He had been catching more fish, but then I just started catching bass, and he could not get a bite. At this point I ought to have had some empathy, but I got prideful. I began to talk "trash." I began to brag that I had caught the last several fish. I now had caught more fish than Gary. Grandkids, you know exactly what happened. I could not get a bite, and my friend began to catch fish consistently. After about an hour or so, he had caught eighteen, and I was stuck at thirteen. I could not even get a nibble. I thought maybe God was trying to teach me a lesson in humility. I actually apologized to Gary and told him that I should have thanked God and given Him the glory. Where I had gone a long time without a bite, I now began to catch fish consistently. During the last hour on the river, I caught ten bass. God blessed me amazingly. I ended up with twenty-three bass, and Gary only caught one more fish. Maybe God really was trying to teach me a lesson.

Another story that I remember began on a Sunday night after church. A few of us were talking about hitting deer with our cars. I had never hit a deer with a car. I had come close many times. I even had a deer jump over the front of my car but had never hit one. It was then that Grandpa said one of the dumbest things he had ever spoken, "Yeah, I do have pretty good reflexes." Instead of bragging on the Lord's goodness, I bragged on my reflexes. That was very ignorant and arrogant on my part. Anybody can hit a deer. One more time you can probably guess what happened. The very next morning my beagle and I were on our way to chase a few bunnies. The problem is that a nice four-point buck decided to "play chicken" with me. That buck crashed into my Lynx and smashed the windshield, dented the hood badly, and scratched the rooftop with its antlers. My reflexes were not quite fast enough. I knew that God was teaching me a lesson the moment that deer hit the car. I have not hit a deer since that infamous morning, and that was over thirty years ago. I have come extremely close many times, but God has been very merciful to me.

The next story happened when I was in tenth grade. I loved football. There were times it just consumed me. Even back when I was walking to grade school, I would pretend to run the ball. I would run to the right and then cut to the left. I would do all these crazy moves and score touchdown after touchdown. If someone was watching me, they probably would have thought that I had lost my mind. I usually zigzagged myself to school every day. I had a reputation for being a "hard hitter" even when I was young. I remember, even in fifth and sixth grades, playing pickup ball and hitting people recklessly. I was not even afraid of the older kids. Everybody wanted me on their team. This continued even when I began to play organized ball in seventh grade in Jackson, Michigan. I loved to run the ball, but I loved even more playing linebacker. In eighth grade the coach made me the "wolf man." He allowed me to play anywhere I wanted on defense. I could roam the field. Of course, I always keyed on the opponents' best player.

In ninth grade we moved to Evart, Michigan. I was the only ninth grader with any organized football experience. This was before Evart had organized ball for younger kids. This experience definitely gave me an advantage over my teammates. I was moved up to the Junior Varsity team. I was a running back and linebacker. Before the end of the football season, I was asked to play on the varsity team. I stayed on Junior Varsity, because it was so much fun. We only lost one game that year, and we were having a blast. The problem that occurred was that many people began to tell me how good I was. I was not only confident, but I got very cocky. I let their compliments go straight to my head. The next year I was the only tenth grader on Varsity. I was starting at running back and linebacker. I was also very arrogant and full of pride, thinking that I was one of the best football players in Michigan. I did not give God any praise. I knew I was good and that nobody could stop me. Grandkids, this was not a good way to be. Enjoy sports, play hard, be a team player, and if God blesses you with ability and skill, thank Him. Don't get arrogant, prideful, and full of self.

One night Evart was having its annual Blue and Gold Game. Now they scrimmage other schools, but back then they still had an inter-squad scrimmage. This game was a big deal to the players. We played under the lights and lots of townspeople attended. My number was three, and I wore Puma cleats. That is the last night that I ever wore Pumas; Grandpa is a bit superstitious. I was running the ball off right tackle and cut to the outside. I planted my left cleat, and one of the smallest guys on the team hit me on my lower left leg. Grandpa had dished out an awful lot of pain to others in football but was now lying on his back, writhing in pain. It felt like my left knee had exploded. The doctor later said that I had shredded my ligaments in my knee and that my parents should never allow me to play organized sports again. I was devastated. I had a cast on my leg from my upper hip to the tip of my toes. That cast was on for three months. My world sure unraveled. The doctor said that it was the worst high school injury he had ever seen. It was a long and hard road to recovery, but finally I could walk without crutches. Your great-grandpa and great-grandma allowed me to choose whether I played sports after that. I did choose to play baseball and also played my last two years of football. I did okay. I played third base and batted over .300 in baseball. I was actually all-conference on offense and defense in football. I was honorable mention all-state at linebacker both my junior and senior years. Did I have fun? Yes, but I never played with the joy and reckless abandon that I played with before surgery. I played with a fear that I might hurt that knee and maybe have severe issues with my mobility in the future. There is one more thing. I absolutely loved running the ball and scoring touchdowns. I never ever ran the ball again. I became a blocker for other running backs. Even though I had a dream to play football in college and received letters to play football in college, I never even considered it. My knee was just too bad.

Grandkids, you might be tempted to ask why God was so mean to me. I asked that same question. I did not understand why. I was praying when I was nineteen years old and a freshman in college. While praying, I was questioning God as to why He had allowed my knee to get injured. I had been searching for the answer since I was fifteen years old. It was like suddenly I had a vision in my mind, and I saw a gigantic "P." God somehow spoke to me that the "P" stood for the horrible pride that I had, and He allowed this to happen because of His love for me. He wasn't being mean and nasty, but kind and merciful. Who knows where my pride and arrogance would have led me? God was only saving me from self and myself. I should have been thankful and humbled that God had given me the ability to play ball, but I chose to become a very prideful person.

My left knee has bothered me most of my life. When I played basketball or walked down mountains, etc., my knee would hurt. This was just God's friendly reminder to always give Him the praise and recognition for anything that I accomplished. I had that knee replaced when I was fifty-eight years old. My doctor told me it was the worst knee he had ever replaced. Be very careful to give God the praise when you make a three-pointer, catch a nice smallmouth bass, score a goal in soccer, or kill a nice buck. When you accomplish something, feel satisfied for a job well done, but let others brag on you. You brag on God! Let your grandpa and grandma brag on you. It might be okay to brag a little bit if you win at Rook or Acey-Deucy, though!

"Surely goodness and mercy shall follow me all the days of my life: and I will dwell in the house of the LORD for ever."

PSALM 23:6 (KJV)

THE STORM

The weather can be very unpredictable in Michigan. It can be beautiful and pleasant, and then the wind picks up, and a storm hits. This is a story that happened on Chippewa Lake. Grandma and Grandpa lived in the original homestead that was built on a hill on the west side of the lake. Your grandma's family were some of the first people to settle on Chippewa Lake. Probably another fact that you are not aware of is that your grandma had family who came over on the Mayflower in 1620. They were Edward Fuller, his wife whose name may have been Anne, and their son, Samuel. Their older son, Matthew, came to America later. There was also a Dr. Samuel Fuller who was Edward's brother. Both Edward and his wife died that first year, and Dr. Samuel Fuller raised his nephew, Samuel. Wow! That is pretty cool history. Those Pilgrims were strict, but they also wanted to serve their God unrestricted by government.

To get on with my story, Grandpa and his beagle, Scrambles, went fishing on a beautiful clear day. There was not a cloud in the sky, and the wind was minimal. Scrambles was the first dog that Grandma and Grandpa purchased after we were married. Don't faint, but he was actually a house dog and didn't have to live out in a dog pen like our beagles do now. He became a good rabbit dog but was also a well-trained pet. This is kind of crazy, but Scrambles was one of the main attractions when we had a Sunday school in our home in Mecosta. When we would sing "Jesus Loves Me," I would bring him up front with me. Scrambles would put his head back and howl like a crazy dog. The kids loved it! I would haul several loads of kids in our small Ford Fiesta and pack our living room with about thirty kids every Sunday morning. I remember looking out over those children and realizing that my kids were the only ones in attendance who did not come from a broken home. It broke our hearts but also kept us very motivated to minister to the needy children. Everyone needs Jesus!

This day Scrambles and I were out on Chippewa Lake fishing out of an old, rotting wooden boat. It leaked badly, but I had used it before and made it back to shore. This was one of the boats that Grandma's grandfather used to rent out. He also had a campground and rented four cottages, as well as many boats. Again, it was a very pleasant day, and I was catching a few bluegills. Suddenly the sky darkened, and the wind began to blow. I frantically tried to row back to shore, but because the wood was rotted, the oarlock broke. Before I knew it, I had been blown out to the middle of the lake. Scrambles and I were holding on for dear life. I was holding on to both sides of the boat, trying to keep from capsizing. The waves were so high that they were spilling over the sides of the boat. Grandkids, did I mention that I had no lifejacket? For whatever reason, we never used lifejackets back then. Pretty stupid, I'd say! In the middle of the storm, I did the only thing that I could do. I prayed loudly and fervently to my God and hoped that my beagle and I would not drown. The rain and waves were so blustery that I could not see where we were being blown. I could not even see the shoreline. Poor Scrambles just sat there quietly as the boat filled with water, and the waves continued to cascade over the side. I don't know for sure how long we rode out that storm, but it seemed an eternity. How time flies when you are having fun, but I honestly just thought that the boat was going to sink! The water level kept getting higher and higher in the boat. I just kept praying and holding on. We were in God's hands. The storm continued to rage, but I heard a grating sound. It was music to my ears, and I was filled with relief. The boat had gone aground. Thank the Lord! The wind was howling, and the rain was pouring, but I was rejoicing. I believe we ended up somewhere on the east side of the lake. Terra firma never felt better. Scrambles and I found the road and walked home soaking wet but very happy.

Grandkids, this story was true and frightening. You may never face an actual storm as Grandpa did, but you will encounter storms in your lifetime. There will be circumstances you don't understand. There are life battles and spiritual battles. Those are not the times to quit, give up, or run from the situations. Cry out to God in desperation and endeavor to get a grip on your emotions. Ride out the storm, and eventually you will hit the shoreline.

"And the boat was already a considerable distance from land, buffeted by the waves because the wind was against it. Shortly before dawn Jesus went out to them, walking on the lake. When the disciples saw Him walking on the lake, they were terrified. 'It's a ghost,' they said, and cried out in fear. But Jesus immediately said to them: 'Take courage! It is I. Don't be afraid.' 'Lord, if it's you,' Peter replied, 'tell me to come to you on the water.' 'Come,' he said. Then Peter got down out of the boat, walked on the water and came toward Jesus. But when he saw the wind, he was afraid and, beginning to sink, cried out, 'Lord, save me!' Immediately Jesus reached out His hand and caught him. 'You of little faith,' he said, 'why did you doubt?' And when they climbed into the boat, the wind died down. Then those who were in the boat worshipped Him, saying, 'Truly you are the son of God.'"

MATTHEW 14:24–33 (NIV)

The storms of life will come; don't be captivated by the waves, but keep your eyes on Jesus. The situation may have caught you, but not Jesus, by surprise. Keep the faith, and never ever give up.

NAIN

Grandkids, you are probably wondering what in the world the title of this story means. The word "Nain" probably has no significance to you, but it has great significance to Grandpa. It is found once in the Bible. It was a village in Galilee where Jesus brought the widow's son back to life. The word means "beauty and pleasantness." This was the first documentation of Jesus raising someone from the dead. The Nain that I am writing about was a little Free Methodist church that was several miles from Fairmont, West Virginia. It was way out in the country on a narrow, winding road. Just like the widow's son, Nain was being raised from the dead. It had been closed for many years, and now your great-grandpa was trying to resurrect this church. It was just a small church that had a leaky roof, was very dusty, and needed many repairs. Your great-grandpa and great-grandma were not discouraged. They just started cleaning and repairing. I don't remember how long this process took, but my hunch is that it didn't take long. Your great-grandpa was not the most patient man in the world and was rather driven at times. He had faith that God was going to help them at this church.

In the spring of 1964, they had their first service. There were only five people at that service: three teenagers from the community, Great-Grandpa, and Grandpa. I don't remember anything about that service except for one thing, and that was a girl named Sue got saved. Soon after that, another teenager named Ernie got saved. I can still remember Ernie telling Great-Grandpa that God had saved him, and he had to tell his family. He got up from the altar, walked out of the church, and began running down that country road toward his home. I saw that with my own eyes. Ernie running down that road has been indelibly stamped on my mind. Most of Ernie's family eventually also got saved. I can't remember if Ernie's dad got saved, but I remember him coming to church. Let me tell you the story of how it happened. Of course, the church had been praying, and Great-Grandpa had visited this man occasionally. He had made a connection. I remember on this particular day that they were pitching horseshoes at Ernie's home. Now your great-grandpa was a very competitive person, and he was an excellent horseshoe pitcher. He could throw a ringer just about any time he really concentrated. Great-Grandpa and Ernie's dad began playing a game. Ernie's dad was a good pitcher, and Great-Grandpa challenged him that if he won the game, Ernie would come to church. Great-Grandpa threw lots of ringers and doubles, and the man came to church. Some of those ringers were probably divinely directed. Now we realize that a person does not have to go to church to get saved, but when God is moving in a service, and people have prayed, there is a tendency for people to have their hard hearts softened, and a longing for God is planted in their hearts by the Holy Spirit. There were many, many people who sought God in that small church and found Jesus.

People began to pray and fast, and the Holy Spirit moved in that community in a powerful manner. Many people were saved and healed, and the supernatural acts of God almost became customary instead of the unusual. It was normal during this time that churches would have a week or possibly two weeks of a prearranged revival. At Nain we just kept having church every night. The Spirit of God would come in waves, and people would just praise God spontaneously. Then conviction would settle down on the service, and needy people would seek God at the altar. People would begin to praise God again, and the Holy Spirit's Presence would fill that church. Some people would raise their hands, others would quietly praise God, while some would loudly praise God. Then there might be someone out in the aisles praising God. I remember one evening service where there were three different altar calls. Grandkids, we had services for seven straight weeks. I mean forty-nine straight nights during the school year. I remember Great-Grandpa telling people that the church would pray that the children would not be tired the next day, and we were not—at least I wasn't, and I never missed a service.

I did have to stand outside once, observing the service through an open window. There was no room in the church to sit down. It was that packed many times. People heard how God was moving, and they just came to the services. There were some really good people who came, and others who weren't. They were rather fanatical in certain beliefs and brought division. Sometimes people brought "wildfire." Instead of allowing God to move and work, they did things in the "flesh." Grandkids, when God is working supernaturally, many times Satan will try to undermine God's plan and ways. Satan tries to counterfeit and deceive people. Unfortunately, people are not always discerning and can be led astray.

This church made a commitment that they wanted to see at least one person saved each week. The church would pray, fast, and believe that God would answer that prayer. That prayer was answered week after week. At least one person was saved. I remember one particular Sunday night after the evening service. We came home from church, and your great-grandfather was troubled. The church had seen no new converts that week. He just did not understand. He had prayed, the church had prayed, and nobody had gotten saved. However, it wasn't midnight yet, so there was still time, and my dad had not lost faith. Grandkids, what do you think happened? Yep, you are right one more time. I remember the phone ringing and some unsaved person wanted to talk with my dad. He needed Jesus. Great-Grandpa and Great-Grandma got into the car, drove to their house, and another person got saved. Can you imagine fifty-two straight weeks with at least one person getting saved? Sometimes several people were saved during the week. What spiritual tenacity those people had!

After seeing so many people saved, it was necessary to have a baptismal service. I remember someone counted sixty-three cars parked down by the Tygart River. It is amazing that that many cars travelled down that narrow, winding road. Your grandpa was baptized that day and possibly some of my sisters. After I was baptized, I climbed up into a tree and watched many, many people get immersed. This was not a short service. All those who were baptized needed to testify that Jesus had saved them from their sins. Baptism was an outward sign of an inward work. Not everyone was happy that day. There was an elderly gentleman who was very upset that his elderly wife was getting baptized. He came to church that morning with a cane to beat up Great-Grandpa. I still remember him down by the river raising his cane and shaking it toward Great-Grandpa, and testifying how he was going to beat on the preacher. God convicted him, and he was saved, so he and his wife were baptized together. What a wonderful story of God's grace and mercy! I heard it with my own ears and saw it with my own eyes. This is all firsthand information.

I recall coming to church on a Sunday morning, and a teenage girl was absent. People did not miss church back then unless there was a legitimate reason. I don't remember her name, but she was in Fairmont General Hospital with meningitis. Normally when a person is sick or afflicted, they come to the front of the church and are anointed with oil by the pastor. I don't remember for certain, but I think Great-Grandma Kretoski was anointed for her. The church people gathered around her and prayed fervently with faith. The teenage girl was healed miraculously that very moment. God honored their faithful prayer.

Your grandpa was very privileged to see God save people and work supernaturally many, many times. I witnessed a true revival. Your great-grandpa not only was a tremendous soul winner, but he had the gift of healing. Many were healed when he prayed for them. He wasn't the Healer, but God used him as a connector to God. His faith helped others to have faith and truly believe that God was able to heal them.

Grandkids, this is just a small part of what transpired at Nain. There are still many people who were changed by God there who continue to serve God today. My sisters, your aunts, were also there. I am sure that they may have their own stories and perceptions. One thing for certain, Grandpa saw many supernatural miracles of God and many lives changed. It was God working, not man. Someday Grandpa will die and go to Heaven, but the God who was so evident at Nain is still alive and willing to work in people's lives today. Never lose faith in God, but also be willing to pray and fast. Grandkids, you can also see God move in miraculous ways.

"Jesus Christ is the same yesterday, today, and forever."

HEBREWS 13:8 (NKJV)

UNCONDITIONAL LOVE

Grandkids, Grandpa has already written the story about how we acquired Curly. Remember, he was the dog that we thought was half beagle and half cocker spaniel. He was the size of a beagle and had long, curly, reddish hair. I thought he was beautiful. We bonded immediately, and he became my best friend. What Curly did not know is that I needed a best friend. I was the new kid at school and really had no close friends in the neighborhood. Another thing that really bothered me is that I had become rather chubby, and the neighborhood kids began calling me "Porky." Of course, I acted as if it did not bother me, but deep inside my heart, it hurt me greatly. My family never mentioned my being overweight, but several people outside my home were mean and nasty. The name Porky still causes pain in my heart to this day. I guess I never really got past it. Grandkids, you may be the first people who I have ever discussed this with, other than Grandma. It is about time that I became vulnerable since I am sixty-three years old as I write this story.

It is so important to be very sensitive to the differences in people. Children and even adults can be rude and crude, and make hurtful remarks to others. So often, people will not show their hurt and pain, but deep inside their hearts they are very sad. Be very careful never to make demeaning and offensive remarks to others who may be different or have oddities. I worked with a boy who was gay. Do I think that that lifestyle is sinful and wrong? Most definitely! I always treated this boy with respect and love. I would greet him with a hug when he came to school and when he left. Yes, I did talk with him about God's grace and deliverance. We had friendly but frank discussions pertaining to the Bible. None of this would have happened without me caring and respecting him. You don't always have to agree with people or their lifestyles, but you still need to be kind and considerate, even to your brothers and sisters! Why is all of this so important? People need to see Jesus in us and feel His love.

Let me continue with Curly's story. It was during this time when I became very active in sports, and the excessive chubbiness just seemed to melt off my body. My beautiful dog could not care less if I was fat, skinny, black, white, or even Polish. He just accepted me for who I was. We were best friends, and he had become part of the Kretoski family. He loved us all, but I had a special relationship with him. Though I had unconditional love from my family, I like to think that God knew I needed unconditional love from a friend. We had Curly for thirteen years. If there are dogs in Heaven, and there might be, Curly may be running rabbits with Great-Grandpa right now. Wow! Grandpa has a crazy imagination when he lets his mind wander, but Grandkids, it might be spot on. The Bible tells us that we really can't even comprehend how magnificent Heaven will be.

"A man that hath friends must shew himself friendly: and there is a friend that sticketh closer than a brother."

PROVERBS 18:24 (KJV)

THE BIG ONE THAT
DID NOT GET AWAY

All of my grandkids know that Grandpa is an avid fisherman. Smallmouth bass are my favorite fish to catch. They fight ferociously, and they are not too finicky when it comes to biting. They taste as good as walleye if fixed properly. Now your great-grandfather evolved into mainly a panfish fisherman in his later years. They were not only fun to catch, but also great table fare. He caught hundreds and probably thousands of them, and never grew tired of it. In the springtime he would catch a large mess of fish in the morning and then spend a couple of hours filleting them. He then would do the same thing in the afternoon. He did this day after day. A large mess of fish meant filling a five-gallon bucket almost to the top. At this time there were no limits on panfish in West Virginia, and Great-Grandpa filled his freezer with the bluegill fillets. He did this for many years, and it never seemed to jeopardize the bluegill population. Your great-grandma and great-grandpa were renowned for their fried fish. It seemed that everyone who ever visited them were served a bluegill meal. I have spoken with people years after your great-grandparents went to Heaven, and often they have mentioned those bluegill dinners. The biggest bluegill your great-grandpa ever caught was thirteen and a half inches long. That is huge! I saw that fish with my own eyes, and it was a whopper.

Your grandpa has caught his share of large fish, but I have also lost some giant fish. I remember when Sam and I were fishing under a large bridge, and I felt a strike and set the hook. My ultralight St. Croix pole bent severely, and my reel just screamed as the line was stripped out. That monster fish began to pull the boat downstream, and I hung on for dear life. I tightened my reel three times, and it continued to get stripped out. Finally after what seemed like forever, the fish stopped and just shook its head for a while. Suddenly it took off like a wild torpedo, and there was no stopping it. It headed straight for a large wood pile, and the line did not stop until that fish went under it. My line was tight, but there was no fish on the end of it. It had stripped out probably close to seventy yards of braided line. We motored to the wood pile, and there was my tube bait stuck in a log. We don't really know what type of fish it was, but I am guessing it was a very large catfish.

I remember another time when I was wet-wading the Muskegon River. This is actually my favorite method to fish. I would just become part of the environment and get in my own little world. All the cares of life would evaporate, and my spirit was invigorated. It was just the river, God, and smallmouth bass. It does not get much better than that. A person needs to be very careful while wading a river. It is easy to slip on rocks and logs, or wade into water over your head. I slipped off a rock pile once and got sucked under into very deep water, and found it very difficult to swim one handed out of that swirling water. I did not want to lose my pole. After being sucked under twice, I made it to an island safely where I tried to get my breath and thanked God for His assistance. On this particular evening I caught forty smallmouth. You might ask me how I can remember, but I just do. I caught over twenty-five fish that were over sixteen inches that evening. My first fish was nineteen and one half inches long. I wanted to stretch him to twenty inches but couldn't. I remember fishing some structure and catching four bass on four consecutive casts. I have done that several times, but I have never caught fish that big. The first fish was eighteen inches, and the second was bigger. The third bass was nineteen and one half inches. I caught three very large smallies on three straight casts. I cast out the fourth time and felt the slightest bite. Remember that big fish don't always hit the hardest. Sometimes they just suck it in, and you can barely detect the bite. I set the hook, and things got interesting. I knew that I had hooked into a monster river smallmouth. He was so powerful that he went wherever he chose for several minutes. He went upstream and then downstream. He stripped out line on several occasions. You can't force a large fish. You have to "play" them and tire them out. Finally I tired that fish out and carefully pulled him in my direction. I had him by my side and was reaching for the biggest river smallmouth that I had ever hooked. I did not carry a net when I wet-waded so I was reaching my hand for that fish when he suddenly swam slowly away. The line did not break, but I had tied a bad knot and it unraveled off the tube bait. I just stood there stunned in waist-deep water and watched that twenty-one to twenty-two-inch fish swim away with the tube bait stuck in his lip—one of the big ones that got away. I have hooked into bigger smallmouth on lakes but never on a river.

Let me finish this story with the big one that did not get away. I was eighteen years old and fishing with Great-Grandpa on a small lake near Evart, Michigan. We needed to walk quite a distance to get to the lake and dragged a small rubber raft behind us. We got on the lake, and Great-Grandpa started fishing for panfish, and as usual he began to catch fish. I was fishing with a six- or seven-inch purple worm with three hooks on it that I had attached to a snap swivel. My dad encouraged me to fish for panfish. He wanted fish to eat. I just kept fishing for largemouth bass. I don't remember what order I caught the four bass, but I caught two twenty-one-inchers, one twenty-incher, and a nineteen-incher. Wow, that is quite a stringer of fish, but I needed one more fish to limit out. Today I would probably catch and release such big fish, but back when I was a kid, nobody threw back fish that I can remember. We continued to fish, and Great-Grandpa kept catching panfish, and I kept fishing for bass. Remember how I told you earlier how big fish just suck in the bait. Well, I had a barely discernible bite. It was the smallest of *tunks*, but I set the hook. This was before ultralight poles, but Great-Grandpa and I fished ultralight by putting spinning reels on fly poles. Suddenly that fly pole bent double, and I just hung on for dear life. I knew I could not force the fish and just tried to keep a tight line. When that fish jumped, Grandpa just about "freaked out." It was the biggest bass I had ever laid eyes on. It was huge! In my excitement I still remember hollering, "It's a whale, it's a whale!" Big fish make people say crazy things. All of a sudden that fish swam north and dragged that rubber raft across that small lake until it got the raft wedged against a log that was sticking out of the water. I was sure my line would break as it rubbed against that tree. The next part of this story is going to sound like a lie or an exaggeration, but it is totally the truth with no embellishment. That monster bass jumped out of the water on the opposite side of that tree, but was close to me. I made the catch of my life. I reached out quickly and snatched that fish out of the air. My hand landed in its large mouth, I gripped it, and wrestled it into the raft. I had just caught my largest bass ever! It was twenty-four inches long and eight and a half pounds. I was one happy eighteen-year-old boy. That was one of my big ones that did not get away.

Jesus had a message for His disciples, "And He saith unto them, Follow me, and I will make you fishers of men."

MATTHEW 4:19 (KJV)

It is a fun and wonderful experience to catch a monster fish, but if you lead a person to Jesus, it will be one of the greatest, if not the greatest, that you will ever experience. I hope that each of you will enjoy fishing as long as you live, but how wonderful it will be if each of you will become a fisher of men and women! Grandpa challenges his wonderful grandkids to become soul winners!

LYING TO GREAT-GRANDMA

Grandkids, this might sound like a little white lie, but I never lied to your great-grandpa and only lied to Great-Grandma once. I will tell you the story in a little bit. It seems that in the day that we live, it is okay to lie, cheat, and steal. I have been lied to multitudes of times. It seems that some people are so used to lying that they do it even when it just doesn't make sense. I once had a boy lie to me, because he did not want a shot from the county health nurse. I told him that he needed his rabies shot, and he immediately told me that he had already received it! I just thought that was rather amusing.

Now back to the main story. I had a period in my life, when I was around eleven years old, when I was just plain nasty. I just swore profusely when with my friends or when playing ball. When a stranger drove by me, many times I would give them an obscene gesture. I really don't understand why I did those things. My parents were great examples, and they loved God with all of their hearts. My dad was a pastor, and my mom was a wonderful woman. I can never remember them disciplining me harshly or in anger. That does not mean that I was never spanked. If there was ever a child who deserved to be spanked, it was your grandpa. Great-Grandma spanked me occasionally, but normally it was Great-Grandpa. He would give me a few whacks, and then it was over—at least I wanted it over. Great-Grandpa would always pray for me after I was spanked, and if one of my sisters was involved, we would have to hug and apologize to each other. I was really not in much of a prayerful mood. I really did not get spanked very often and probably not as many times as I deserved. There were a few times when I stuffed a thin paperback book in the back of my pants to lessen the pain. I can remember the very last time your great-grandma spanked me. She used a cloth belt, and I laughed at her. I told her she needed to use a leather belt if she wanted it to hurt. That was one of the dumbest things I have ever said. Her response was that we would just wait for Dad to do the spanking in the future. I remember Great-Grandma sending me to my room for something. I went to my room and climbed out the window, and played with my friends for a while. I then climbed back into my room and knocked meekly on the bedroom door, and asked mom to come out. She was so kind and sweet. She asked me if I was ready to behave, and I, of course, told her I was. She gave me a smile and hug, and off I went. Grandpa is not recommending that his grandkids deceive their parents, but I was rather devious at times. I guess I need to get back to my original story. I had been playing football in the yard of a friend. One of Aunt Vicki's friends walked by and heard all the nasty swearing coming from me. She told Vicki, and Vicki told my mom. Now Great-Grandma was very wise and did not accuse me. She actually spoke to me with tears running down her face. She told me what I had been accused of doing, and that she knew that her boy would never use the Lord's name in vain or use vulgar language. As I looked into that sincere, loving face, my heart felt like it was going to burst. Instead of "manning up" and admitting the truth, I lied. I just could not hurt my mom with the truth. This was my first and only lie to my parents. Can you only imagine how families would be revolutionized if parents would treat their children with tenderness and kindness? There would surely be a lot less anger and rebellion in kids. Grandpa had a little edge to him and at times questioned authority, but I always wanted to please my parents. They loved me unconditionally and were never mean. We did not always agree on everything, and we could be rather inflexible in our thinking, but we always respected each other.

Trust is so important in relationships. Can you imagine if I was always wondering if Grandma was telling me the truth? I have never questioned her honesty. If a person would lie to me once, I would probably have a difficult time ever believing that person totally again. When a person lies, I think that it is easier to lie again. One study showed that the brain becomes desensitized when we lie, so that every time we lie, it becomes easier. Neuroscientists say that the amygdala in the brain actually changes. That is pretty scary stuff.

> "speaking lies in hypocrisy, having their own conscience seared with a hot iron,"
>
> 1 TIMOTHY 4:2 (NKJV)

Here we have a documented study that actually substantiates the Bible. We can always trust the Word of God, but we surely can't trust every scientific study. Grandkids, Grandpa should never have lied to your great-grandma. That was a sin. Also, realize that some people are just nosey and will ask you questions. Don't allow yourself to be manipulated into talking about something when you don't feel comfortable. You may have to tell people that you don't feel right in discussing the situation with them, because it might not be any of their business, and you don't want to gossip. When it comes to your parents or even your grandparents, you need to be totally one hundred percent honest. Now if Grandpa is too nosey, just ask him to back off. Don't ever allow your heart and mind to become desensitized because of lying.

CLOSE CALL

This next story actually happened to Grandpa when he was sixty-two years old, but before I get to that story, I need to mix in a couple of related stories. We have probably all had close calls where we could have been severely hurt or even lost our lives. I remember once when Great-Grandpa and I were going to go catfishing on Buffalo Creek. Now Buffalo Creek is not a little stream but a full-sized river. Before Great-Grandpa and I would go catfishing, we would go to Paw Paw Creek or another creek and catch crawdads. Sometimes we would go during the daytime, but often at night. I can still see your great-grandpa sliding his hand gently into the water behind the crawdad, then moving his hand slowly until he was close, and then quickly snatching that crab, normally just behind the head. He would either put it into a minnow bucket that was strapped to him or into a minnow bucket that I was carrying. He would almost always snatch a soft-shell or double-shelled crab. He had caught so many crabs over the years that he could tell by their color if they were hard- or soft-shelled. A soft-shell crab is one that has recently molted or lost its hard shell because it needs to grow. A double-shelled crab is one that is in the process of molting but has not lost its hard shell yet. A soft-shell crab is probably the best bait ever for catfish or smallmouth bass. One reason Great-Grandpa caught so many fish is that he took time to catch the right bait. I never developed the savvy to only catch the soft-shell crabs. I would latch onto a hard-shell crab most of the time. I have flung many crawdads off my fingers as they snipped me with their sharp pinchers. When we caught crabs at night, we would use a lantern or a strong light. There would be more crabs out then, because they are predominantly nocturnal. Sometimes Great-Grandpa and I would see two gleaming eyes staring at the light when closer to shore. Great-Grandpa would sneak near those eyes and grab a big bullfrog. I really did not like to catch crabs at night. Remember, I did not have waders on but a pair of cutoff jeans and tennis shoes. Grandkids, I think you probably know the main reason why I got nervous at night. Copperheads! I was always thinking about those nasty snakes. On this particular night we had gotten plenty of crabs and were driving to Buffalo Creek. We did not drive the normal route but took a shortcut. We were driving slowly down a two-track when Great-Grandpa suddenly hit the brakes. He told me that something was not right, and that he had an impression of danger. We both got out of the car, and one of us had a flashlight. We shined the flashlight to find that we were just a few feet from a cliff with the river about one hundred feet down below. That was very scary, but we were thankful that Great-Grandpa listened to God's warning. God did not speak audibly but yet very distinctly to Great-Grandpa's heart. We were probably only a half of a second from driving over that cliff and into the water.

Another time God protected Grandma. We had probably been married for a couple of years, and we were both in Big Rapids. We drove separately for some reason. I can't remember why, but I do remember following her home. We had just turned east on Chippewa Lake Road and were nearing the railroad tracks. It is now a biking and walking trail. Grandma was a short distance from the tracks when I saw the train. I was waiting to see her brake lights come on. She just kept driving and was oblivious to the train. I was screaming for her to stop and was sure I was going to witness my beautiful wife getting smashed by that train. I was screaming and praying in those few short seconds as she drove over the tracks. Her car disappeared from my view, because the train entered the intersection. I was rejoicing and thanking God, because I did not think that Grandma got hit. I don't think that she even knew that she was almost run over by a train. I was trembling and almost had a nervous breakdown. God had extended His mercy one more time to the Kretoski family. Grandpa's opinion is that many times in this life we receive God's protection and are oblivious to any danger. Sometimes we get aggravated and impatient when we are delayed from getting somewhere, while it could be God's providence and protection. Yes, Grandkids, I do believe in guardian angels, also.

Grandpa used to drive very fast. It's one thing to be in an emergency situation, but Grandpa was just stupid for driving like he did. When I became a daddy, I slowed down some, and then as I grew older I continued to drive slower. Now I usually just drive like a grandpa and try not to be harried. I was twenty or twenty-one and was in my first year of marriage. I was on Route 46 near Cedar Springs, driving at least ninety miles per hour. I then pulled into the parking area near our trailer. I was ready to walk into the house when I heard a rather loud explosion. My passenger front tire had just blown out. Can you imagine if I would have been traveling ninety miles per hour? Grandpa was really careless, but God was really merciful. There is an antiquated cliché that says that "speed kills," and it is absolutely true. When you are able to drive, don't text or speed!

Grandkids, here is one more short story. I had just left my sister Carol's house and had driven to Spring Arbor to pick up Greg at his sister's home. Now we were driving back to Evart in my old, green '69 Galaxie 500. We were driving down Route 60 close to Moscow Road. Cars had slowed down in the other lane to turn left onto Moscow. I was probably driving sixty to sixty-five. The first car turned left, and that was okay. I remember insinuating to Greg that the next car had better not turn left. You guessed it; it turned smack dab in front of us. That car was broadside, and there were cars in the other lane. I don't remember what we said, but I reflexively slammed on the brakes, turned the steering wheel one way and then back the other way, and we zigzagged between those cars. There is absolutely no way that I could have guided that car through those cars. Greg and I should have had a major accident and could have been injured or even killed. I take no credit for driving us between those cars. It was God Who miraculously protected two teenage boys. We were so full of excitement and adrenaline after that "close call." In a few minutes we turned onto East 94, and the seriousness of this near accident hit me. My body felt weird, and my legs started shaking uncontrollably. I was eighteen and had never lost control of my body. That sounds kind of crazy but is true.

As I said earlier, this next story happened when I was sixty-two years old. I was visiting a kid who had left Pineview. I would visit kids at their homes or school and endeavor to counsel them to continue to make positive choices. If they were having difficulty, I would attempt to enhance their coping skills and to increase their chances of being successful on the "outs." I would also usually pray with them and encourage them to seek Jesus for salvation and strength. It really does take Jesus to break the "wicked cycle" of dysfunctional families and self-destructive behavior. I was driving along in my own little "Grandpa's world." I just think about my family, big smallmouth bass, big bucks, church situations, etc., and sometimes I just worship God as I travel. My mind travels from A to Z. Now, normally when I come to railroad tracks, I slow down and look in both directions at least twice. That day I was in "Grandpa's world" and driving carefully but did not really pay attention to the railroad tracks. It almost cost me my life. I drove over the tracks, heard a noise, and looked into my rearview mirror. The only thing I saw was a train. I hadn't seen it and hadn't heard it, but I was also not looking for it. I was really not paying attention. I probably came within one half of a second to getting smashed by a train. One more time God extended His mercy to me, and I was so very thankful. It sure brought back a previous memory that had occurred forty years earlier on Chippewa Lake Road.

"Why, you do not even know what will happen tomorrow. What is your life? You are a mist that appears for a little while and then vanishes."

JAMES 4:14 (NIV)

Grandkids, don't take life for granted. I'm not trying to scare you, but you can be here today and be in eternity tomorrow. This quote used to be popular when Grandpa was a kid: "Only one life 'twill soon be past, only what's done for Christ will last." That is still true for today. Abraham Lincoln said, "It's not the years in your life that count; it's the life in your years." I hope that all my grandkids grow up to be wonderful people full of vision, enthusiasm, and passion. I also hope that at the core of your life is Christ. Life will have its "close calls," but don't allow that to hinder you from living life with "gusto"!

BULLIES

When I was little, I got into many fights. I hated to be pushed around, and I detested bullies. Your great-grandpa always admonished me as a young kid not to fight. He just wanted me to have a different and better life than he had had. He wanted me to turn the other cheek. I would come home from school or someplace where I had just gotten the tar beat out of me. I remember once walking down our street, and two guys who were in middle school or maybe even high school jumped me. Remember, Grandpa was only seven or eight when this situation occurred. This was not the first time these guys had bullied me. One would hold my arms behind my back, and the other guy would hit me in the stomach. I did not reveal this information, because they had threatened to kill me and my family if I told anyone. I lived in fear for several weeks. My stomach was hurting me, probably from a combination of getting hit and anxiety. On this particular day these guys started pounding me too close to home. Aunt Vicki or Aunt Carol happened to look out a window and saw their little brother getting the snot beat out of him. They both ran out of the house and jumped the top railing of the porch. They ran to my rescue and whipped the tar out of those two guys as they screamed and hollered. They then told the other students at their school how those two boys had beaten and bullied their little brother. Those two boys received unimaginable ridicule and were humiliated for a long time. Grandkids, people reap what they sow. In this case the reaping may have been worse than the sowing. At any rate, I would not fight back.

After this happened a few times, Great-Grandpa told me that I had the right to protect myself and actually taught me how to fight. He told me to never start a fight, and if he ever found out that I had, he would spank me. I can honestly say that I have never started a fight. Great-Grandpa also told me that if you have to fight, then get the first punch in. If the other person starts it, and you know you can't get out of it, hit him hard. Unfortunately, I had to do this many times growing up. Grandkids, after reading this, I don't ever want you to think that Grandpa is advocating that you fight—just the opposite. Fight for peace. Fighting is absolutely a last resort, and hopefully none of my grandkids will ever have to physically fight a person. Always remember that a kind, soft, and gentle word decreases anger. Never allow your anger to be your dictator or to control you. Don't lash out at people and escalate an angry situation. I am not glorifying fighting, but I am going to write about a few situations when I had to protect myself. Every one of the examples happened when I was in sixth grade. I never got in another fight after sixth grade. Thank the Lord!

It seems that there has to be a pecking order in many schools. It was no different at State Street School. This particular school went from first grade through eighth grade. Again, I was in sixth grade and had not attended this school for very long. A kid named Danny was the toughest kid in sixth grade. He was mean and a bully, and most kids were afraid of him. It was during lunchtime when he tried to prove his dominance over me. We were playing basketball, and he kept ramming into me and pushing me. I can actually remember trying to talk with him and calm him down. He just wanted to show that he was tougher than me. All the kids gathered around us, and we got into our fighting stance. I still tried to persuade him to be my friend and not to fight. He would not listen; he was a bully. Grandkids, don't think for a minute that I enjoyed fighting. I did not want to get hit, but I was too proud to run. Danny wanted me to cower, but I refused. I was not arrogant and was not talking "trash," but my adrenaline was pumping. We were circling each other, and I knew that he probably thought I was going to try to hit him in the face. I faked like I was going to hit him in the face, and he brought his hands up to protect it. I then hit Danny in the stomach with every ounce of power that I had. The air swooshed out of him, and he doubled over with pain. The kids were screaming and yelling. I think they were glad that a bully got whipped. I could have pounded him in the face at this point but actually just wanted it to be over and done. I began to walk away toward the school, and guess who I saw? There stood Mr. Stanley, the principal of the school. He told the crowd to disperse and walked Danny and Grandpa to his office. He was not in the mood to listen to my story. Yes, I hit Danny very hard, but in my mind I was innocent. I was protecting myself just like Great-Grandpa had taught me. Mr. Stanley looked at us boys and reached for his gigantic wooden paddle. He told us to bend over, and we bent over. He proceeded to give each of us several very hard whacks on our rears. He had no mercy. We then stood up and faced him. He said menacingly, "I don't want boys fighting in my school." I can still see his face with that big Italian nose as he sent us back to class. Things were a little different back in 1966. Was it fair that Grandpa got spanked? Probably not, but life is not always fair. We have got to learn to roll with the punches or maybe even the whacks.

This next incident happened after my fight with Danny, with a kid who was in seventh grade. I can see him in my mind, and I think his name was Gene. I will call him Gene in this story. He was a big kid, heavyset, and he, too, was a bully. This incident also started on the same basketball court during lunch again. Gene started pushing me around and calling me names. I did not want to fight and actually walked away from the court. Some kids thought I was scared and was running away. The stupid guy stalked me up to the school. I finally stopped walking and just stood there. He was calling me a sissy and other names. I told him I did not want to fight. There was no reason to fight. Gene was overconfident and loved the attention as a large crowd of kids encircled us. I had no choice but to fight and protect myself. We were circling each other in our fighter's stance, and Gene was so arrogant. He actually thought I was a coward.

I did the same thing to him that I had done to Danny. I acted like I was going to hit him in the face, and he swallowed it hook, line, and sinker. He quickly moved both fists up to guard his face. It was too late for Gene. I hit him in his big belly with every ounce of strength I had. He doubled over in pain, and I could have beat his face to a pulp, but I chose to walk away. As he labored to breathe, I heard him say that we would meet after school and finish this fight. I was thinking that maybe I should have just beat the "living snot" out of him while he was gasping for air and all doubled over. The poor guy was so embarrassed and humiliated that he was just trying to save face with the milling mob. Again, I think the school kids were happy that I took another bully down. I was happy that Mr. Stanley did not bust me fighting again. I did not like that big wooden paddle. It was a nerve-wracking afternoon in school. I found it very hard to concentrate. I did not know what I would encounter after school. I remember walking down the cement school steps and was on high alert for Gene. He was nowhere in sight. I walked home, but Great-Grandpa realized something was wrong with me and questioned me. I told him what had transpired. He asked me if I knew where Gene lived, and I told him I did. Great-Grandpa said that we were going to the house to visit with Gene and his parents. I was mortified. There was no way that I wanted to take my dad to see Gene. There was no arguing with Dad, so I apprehensively got into the car. We drove to the house, and Great-Grandpa went and knocked on the door. Gene's mother came to the door, and Great-Grandpa explained why he was there. Eventually, three or four brothers joined their mother out in the front yard, and I was sure that there was going to be a major confrontation. However, Grandpa was surely wrong in this situation. Great-Grandpa just felt compassion for this destitute family. He began to talk to Gene about the fight and how he just wanted us to be friends. Then his pastor's heart went into action. He gently but steadfastly began to talk with them about Jesus and how Jesus loved them, and how He wanted to save and change their family. Great-Grandpa then knelt in the front yard and prayed passionately for their salvation, and that God would help this dear woman to raise her family. When we were leaving, Great-Grandpa told them he would love to pick them up for church. They never came to church, and Gene and I never became best friends, but we never had another altercation. Also, one more time my respect level only increased for my father. Your great-grandpa was a strong, fearless man, but I never observed him displaying a mean or harsh spirit.

This next story will be short. This happened at the basketball court, also. I don't remember this boy's name or why this situation even happened, but I do remember that this kid got angry and turned into a wild maniac. He charged me like a wild animal, so I had no choice but to start swinging at him. This fight ended quickly, because I hit him several times. The problem was that he had crashed into me, and his face hit my face. I don't know how it happened, but he gashed my cheek with his teeth. Blood was running down my face, and I probably looked rather scary. I had a one-inch scar on my upper left cheek for many years. I whipped this guy pretty quickly and never got hit—just bit.

I am actually rather embarrassed concerning this next episode, because I allowed my anger to control my actions and retaliated. My reaction was wrong. I was not protecting myself. This incident occurred in a church service at Mill Fall Run. There was a youth who attended services with his family. He was in tenth grade, and, yes, I was in sixth. He was probably five or six inches taller than I was and was constantly pushing the younger kids around. We were sitting next to each other in a pew, and he pulled the hair on the back of my neck. I slightly overreacted. I busted him right in the "ole kisser" with a left hook and rocked his world. He was shocked, and I was shocked, and I was waiting to hear Great-Grandpa's reprimanding voice. Somehow he did not see it, and no one ever told him. I don't know whether to call it luck or God's mercy. Yes, this kid never messed with me again, but that was not a good enough reason to hit a person in the mouth. Grandkids, always try to be a peacemaker, turn the other cheek, and endeavor to overcome evil with good.

May I talk to you about one more fight on the basketball court? This was my last real fight but also the worst one that I ever fought. I can't remember his first name, but the guy's last name was Kushic, and he was the toughest kid in seventh grade—just a strong, athletic kid. We were playing one-on-one at the infamous basketball court. It was after school, and we were the only kids playing. Kushic became angry, and I don't know why, but he came at me swinging. I had no choice but to protect myself and reciprocated. Most of the fights that I was in were short, but this was a marathon. Both of us were hurt, but both of us were too proud to give up. We just kept hitting each other. I actually knocked him down with a left hook to the face, and he got up and kept fighting. We fought up a knoll and then grabbed each other, and tried to hit each other as we rolled back down the same knoll. We were both exhausted and breathing heavily. I finally had an opening and put him in a headlock. At this point I could hardly talk; I was so dog-tired and struggling to breathe. I told him that we could be friends, or I was just going to begin beating his face in. Kushic, to my relief, said, "Let's be friends," as he gasped for air. That nasty fight was finally over, and we actually became friends. We both stood there looking at each other kind of stupidly. His face was swollen and bruised. I could feel that my face was swollen and bruised, also. We were dirty and totally exhausted but had a mutual respect for each other. I walked home, and there were many questions when I walked into the house. I answered them the best I could and then got cleaned up for supper. Now there was a problem. It was Wednesday. Yes, it was prayer meeting night. In the Kretoski household, we did not miss a church service unless we were really sick or there was some other extenuating circumstance. I went to church with a bruised, swollen, and battered face. My whole body was aching. Grandkids, you would not believe the sarcastic remarks that I heard that night—mainly from the youth, but even a few adults. I just told them that the other guy was worse than I was. Most of them did not believe me.

This fight began because of anger and continued because of pride. There are other reasons why people fight, but those are two of the main reasons why people get into altercations. It normally begins with snide and nasty remarks, and then escalates into a physical confrontation.

Can I tell one more story? Danny was the person who was involved in this story. He was the guy I fought at the beginning. Danny did not like me after our fight and spanking from Mr. Stanley, but he never messed with me again, until this particular afternoon. The trouble was that he still bullied other kids. I was walking up the school's front steps to return to class after lunch, and there was Danny picking on a smaller kid. I did not ignore it; I wanted to help the bullied kid. I stopped Danny, and I can still remember exactly what I said to him: "If you have to pick on someone, pick on me." He explosively slapped me in the face and then ran like a wild rabbit. I took off after him and chased him like a wild dog. Danny was fast, but I was faster. I was closing in for the kill when both of us were grabbed by crosswalk monitors. Where do you think they marched us to? If you guessed Mr. Stanley's office, you are right. I was not too submissive this time. I did not want to be spanked again, and I was still upset with this situation. I didn't give Mr. Stanley time to question us. I just blurted out the story. I'm sure Mr. Stanley could see the handprint on the side of my face and was quite sure he believed my story. Abruptly he looked at Danny and said, "Get out of my school, and don't come back this year." Danny, with his head bowed, walked out of the school dejectedly. This occurred in the spring of the year so there were several weeks of school left. I went to class with no consequence. It was then 1967, and principals surely had a lot of authority.

Grandkids, never ever start a fight. Protect yourself, but don't instigate and aggravate others when they want to fight you, and never ever be a bully. Try to always come to the rescue of someone who is weaker or less fortunate.

"Make every effort to live in peace with everyone and to be holy; without holiness no one will see the Lord."

Hebrews 12:14 (NIV)

Pyromaniac

This story took place when Grandpa was about eight years old, and we lived in Bell, California. Bell was located not too far from Los Angeles. Back in the day, parents did not worry about their kids like they do today. I rode my bike or skateboard just about anywhere I wanted. I used to ride a skateboard to school, hide it in some bushes, and then ride it back home. These skateboards were not fancy like the ones today but were mainly homemade out of two-by-fours. There have always been cruel, abusive, and sadistic people in the world, but it seems that it is much worse today. I remember once as a little boy, I was walking on the sidewalk near an intersection. A group of teenagers was in a car which was stopped at a stop sign. One of the teenagers had a box of wooden matches. He struck the match on the box and flipped it in my direction. The burning match landed on my eye area and burned me rather badly. Fortunately, it did not land directly on my eyeball. I had a major blister right above my eye.

Another time I was riding my bike and three kids began throwing rocks at me. I remember getting hit on the hand and getting my knuckle broken open. After this incident, the Kretoski vengeful spirit raised its ugly head. Though I was just young, I got my payback. I hunted those boys down until I found each of them alone and then whipped them individually. I remember one of the boys cowering and begging me not to hit him, but I still thrashed him. I am sixty-three years old, and I still regret to this day what I did to that kid. The situation worsened when he ended up in the hospital, and I thought it was my fault. He had an appendectomy. After he got out of the hospital, we actually became friends. Grandkids, listen up: it is never ok to get vengeance and retaliate. It is wrong and sinful. Satan took my hurt feelings and pain and manipulated me, and I chose to do wrong. It was a willful decision. The only reason I wrote this story was to show my grandkids the negativism of a vengeful spirit. The Bible teaches that you overcome evil with good. It also teaches that you bless them that curse you and then pray for people that use you in a nasty manner. Protect yourself, but never retaliate. I hate to say this, but there will be times when you will be hurt by others. Never come down to another person's level and lose your self-respect. As individuals, we are always responsible for our actions and attitudes. Never blame others for your behavior. Take ownership.

Wow! Talk about getting distracted and losing focus. Grandkids, there are times my mind goes crazy as I write *Grandpa's Stories*. My mind is going a hundred miles an hour, but my short little stubby Polish fingers can only type so fast. Anyway, I will get back to the original story. When I was little, I loved to play with matches. Grandpa was rather stupid sometimes. On this particular day, a friend and I had ridden behind a large furniture store. The store had large metal bins where they put lots of cardboard. You can probably guess what happened then. My friend and I were playing with matches and thought that all the flames were out. We got out of the bin and rode off on our bikes not realizing that the fire was not out. Soon after we rode off, we heard the sirens. We did not know where the fire was but soon found out. The cardboard in the bin was on fire, and the flames had caught the back of that store on fire. We were absolutely terrified as we watched the firemen spray the back of the store and eventually put the flames out. Even as a little boy, I was so thankful that store did not burn down but was scared out of my wits. I don't ever remember playing with matches again. I did learn my lesson. Were my friend and I being mean and malicious? No, but we were extremely stupid and careless. Did we purposefully start that fire? Of course not, but we were totally responsible for it. God's mercy surely was extended to Grandpa that day. I was so scared about this situation that I never told anyone for years. I eventually told the story to Great-Grandma Kretoski, and she was totally flabbergasted that her sweet, innocent boy could do such a dastardly deed. We were living back in Fairmont, West Virginia, when I told her.

Grandkids, if there is a lesson that I want you to learn from this story, it is this: always think before you act. There are consequences for every action. These consequences can be positive or negative. One unthoughtful act can affect you for a very long time or even for a lifetime.

"Wise people think before they act; fools don't and even brag about their foolishness."

PROVERBS 13:16 (NLT)

Don't be reactionary and allow your emotions to control you. Slow down, think, and pray. Ask yourself what God would want you to do concerning the situation.

SMOKING

Grandkids, your grandpa did not always make good decisions growing up and was rather impulsive at times. I did not always sit back and think about the pros and the cons of my behavior or decisions. I think most kids are similar to that. There will come a point in your maturation where you will need to slow down and ponder your choices. There might be times in your life when you choose an inappropriate role model. I remember an older youth in our community who smoked. This type of behavior is very uncool, but when Grandpa was young, he thought this guy was tough and looked up to him. I remember someone walking down the sidewalk and flipping a mostly smoked cigarette on the sidewalk. I was probably only seven, but I picked that stinking cigarette up and stuck it between my lips. It tasted pathetic and burned my throat, but I choked that first puff down anyway. Suddenly, I heard your great-grandma's voice speaking to me. I can't recall what she said, but there I stood a short distance from her with a smoking cigarette in my trembling hand. I have no idea how Great-Grandma did not see the spiraling smoke, but I quickly put the cigarette behind my back, dropped it, and began walking toward her. To this day I wonder how my sweet mom would have reacted if she actually had seen her sweet, innocent, little boy puffing on a cigarette or had seen it in his hand. It would probably not have been pretty. Did I know smoking was wrong? Absolutely. Even as a young boy I had heard the story of how God delivered Great-Grandpa instantaneously from twenty-four years of smoking. Before he was even saved, under conviction (Have your mom or dad explain what that means.), he felt God condemning him for smoking. Though he had tried and failed many times to quit, he stopped "cold turkey" when he knew it did not please God. When he left for work that day, he tossed his cigarettes to Great-Grandma and told her he would never smoke again. She laughed at him. She had heard that statement before several times and knew he would fail. What she did not understand was the power of the true and living God. When Great-Grandpa committed to stop smoking, God instantaneously delivered him from his addiction. He told me that he started smoking when he was eight years old and smoked until he was thirty-two. From that moment Great-Grandpa told me he never had a "hankering" for another cigarette and never smoked again. That was actually a supernatural act of God. It was during this time of conviction, when Great-Grandpa was feeling guilty for his sinful lifestyle, that he quit, not only smoking, but lying, stealing, drinking, and cheating. Even though he did not understand the process of conviction and repentance, he knew that God was speaking to him and made many changes before he even got saved.

Now just because Great-Grandpa quit did not mean that Great-Grandma followed his example. She continued to smoke. Six months after Great-Grandpa was saved, she was saved and immediately quit smoking. She knew it was sinful and displeased God. Was she immediately delivered from her sinful habit? Absolutely not! She "hankered" and craved cigarettes for up to a year. She told me she even hid cigarettes in the house and desperately wanted to smoke. Grandkids, do you know how many cigarettes your great-grandma smoked during that difficult time? Zero! Where Great-Grandpa was delivered immediately, she had to resist temptation, but with the help of God, she never gave in. Finally after many long months, she, too, found freedom from her addiction. Could God have taken her craving for cigarettes away immediately just like He did for Great-Grandpa? Yes, He could have, but for some reason He chose not. Your great-grandma could then be an encouragement to others who were struggling with an addiction. If people stand strong and resist temptation, they will eventually be totally delivered from their addictions. God will always give strength to those who are struggling with an addiction or a dependence on something, but they can't keep dabbling with it. They should stand strong and fight it, but always be aware that they will fail in their own strength. It takes the help of God to overcome.

There was a book written several years ago called *The Jesus Factor*. The success rate in most rehabilitation programs used to be, I think, between seventeen and twenty-two percent, depending on the length of the rehab. The longer the rehab, the higher the percentage of success. What many people could not understand is how one rehab had a success rate of eighty-six or eighty-seven percent. After much examination they could find only one main difference. Grandkids, can you guess what that one main difference was? It was Jesus. That one rehab enveloped their addicts with Jesus, prayer, and Bible reading. Jesus was and still is the main reason why people find deliverance from addictions and self-destructive behaviors. When people say that they are failures and can't stop doing a certain action or behavior, they are probably right. It takes Jesus to overcome sin and addictions! We usually just can't overcome in our own power. It takes God's power. Does it sound like I'm preaching? My motives are pure. I just want my grandkids to realize that they can overcome anything and everything with the help of God. Nothing is too hard for God. I do understand that there are some people who break their negative behaviors without God, but I also know that there is not a person alive who can live without willfully sinning unless they have God's help and intervention.

Now let me continue with another story about smoking. Again I was only seven or eight years old when this happened. It seems that Satan was trying to get his talons in me at an early age. We still lived in California when both of these stories took place, and we did not move back to West Virginia until I was eight. Grandpa was being rather goofy again. I was with at least one of my parents at the grocery store. They went inside, and someone who was behind them dropped his cigarette just outside the store before he entered. I grabbed that stupid thing and began puffing on it. I was quickly overcome with guilt and shame, and had to get rid of the cigarette. Instead of just tossing it away, I saw a paper bag littered near the store. Grandkids, this story gets really ridiculous now. I dropped the cigarette into the bag, then threw the bag down, and ran back to our old Plymouth station wagon. I had crazily dropped that bag near the entranceway. Here we went again with fire. That bag caught on fire, and one or two people were out in front of the store stomping on the bag, trying to put the fire out. Thank God that was the very last time I smoked a cigarette. I never had a desire to smoke as I grew older. I was rather frightened as those men put out that fire. I never got "busted" that time, either.

I remember your great-grandpa and other preachers preaching that a person should never take the first puff or drink, because then you would never have to stop. I used to think that that was so simple a concept. Later as an adult, I remember reading a book on addiction, and the author said the exact same thing. That little simple concept is really very powerful. If a person never starts, he never has to stop. Don't allow your curiosity to tempt you into ever doing sinful behaviors.

> "Do you not know that your bodies are temples of the Holy Spirit, who is in you, whom you have received from God? You are not your own; you were bought at a price. Therefore honor God with your bodies."
>
> 1 CORINTHIANS 6: 19–20 (NIV)

> "So whether you eat or drink or whatever you do, do it all for the glory of God."
>
> 1 CORINTHIANS 10:31 (NIV)

MUGGED

This is another story that happened out in Bell, California. I had so much freedom as a boy growing up—probably too much. I just kind of did what I wanted to do. I rode my bike, skateboarded, or just walked about wherever I wanted. Again, it was a very different day and age. As an eight- or nine-year-old boy, I ran away several times. I would go to the meat store and buy twenty-five cents' worth of hotdogs. I had a stick that I put over my shoulder with a cloth bundle on the end. I would put those hotdogs in the bundle and start walking. I would not necessarily know where I was going, but I would walk until I ran out of food or got too tired. I would return home, and that episode of running away was over. Thinking back, I have no recollection of why I was running away. I remember once that I wrote a runaway note and left it on the kitchen table. I climbed up in our walnut tree in the backyard just to see what would happen. After a while my sisters (and maybe Great-Grandma) came out on the back porch, hollering and looking for their little brother. I realized then that they did actually love and care for me. I sneakily climbed down out of that tree and made my grand entrance back into the house after a short period of time. I never told them that I had watched them while hiding in that tree. As I reminisce about my behavior growing up, I realize that I was a different child. I'm sixty-three years old as I write this story and am still trying to figure out why I did some of the things I did. Grandkids, I guess your grandpa was just weird. Probably a lot of people still think I am weird, but that is okay. I kind of like weirdness. It is okay to be different. One of the worst things that you can do is to compare yourself with others. There are always going to be people who are smarter, prettier, more handsome, more athletic, or more talented than you—at least maybe. I sure have some smart, good-looking, and talented grandkids. The key is not to compare. Accept who you are, and remember that you were uniquely created in God's image.

I remember walking down one of the main boulevards in Bell. It was a four-lane highway with many big buildings interconnected with each other. I had grown rather leery of people while traipsing around the city. I had had several nasty encounters with people and had developed a cautious mentality when alone. Oftentimes, I would actually cross over to the other side of the street when I saw a group of people or somebody bigger than me. I learned to survive. On this particular day, I was walking down the sidewalk when confronted by a man who was probably in his early twenties. He spoke to me and told me I had stolen one hundred dollars from him. My immature reply was that I only had seventeen dollars on me. Now before you get too critical of my response, remember I was probably only eight or nine years old. He very boldly told me to give him the seventeen dollars. I adamantly refused, and he lunged for me. I can still remember his arm going over my head and me squirming away like a wild child. I was terrified and fighting for my life—maybe literally. I don't really know how far I was from home, but it was quite a distance. He chased me for a short distance, but my short, little Polish legs were running faster than they had ever run before. I sprinted all the way home in my fear. When I finally got to the house, I was laboring for breath convulsively. When I saw Great-Grandma, I had a major meltdown. I was trembling and crying with great sobs. I had just been traumatized. Great-Grandma kept asking me what happened, and I could not respond yet. She just held me, talked soothingly, and patted on me. I knew I was safe. I eventually got my breath and calmed down enough to tell my mom what had happened. Then she cried with me. She was extremely thankful that her sweet and innocent little boy was safe and sound, although I really don't know how sound. It took a long time for me to heal from that traumatic experience. I was extremely careful and cautious when I went traipsing around the community after that.

Wow! That was rather exciting and scary at the same time. Grandkids, God Almighty surely listened to the prayers of Great-Grandpa and Great-Grandma. I'm quite sure that my guardian angel had to work overtime while protecting me. Scary things may happen to us, but we can't live in a constant state of anxiety and fear. In time we must move on and continue to trust Jesus. Now I know that we live in a rather negative society. There are good people, and there are bad people. Hopefully, there are many more good than bad, but because of the bad people, we need always to be mindful of our surroundings and be careful. Let me give you an example. When we lived in Muskegon, I liked to walk down the streets of Muskegon Heights and talk with people and browse through different pawn shops, etc. When I did this, it was always late morning or early afternoon. Muskegon Heights is similar to a little Detroit. There are lots of crime and violence. I would have been foolish to do the very same thing at night. Don't let your impulsive nature lead you into risky areas. Use your head for more than a hat rack.

"The Lord will rescue me from every evil assault, and He will bring me safely into His Heavenly kingdom; to Him be the glory forever and ever. Amen."

2 TIMOTHY 4:18 (AMP)

THE HIT

Grandkids, have you ever wondered where dreams come from? Now your Grandpa has had some of the wackiest-of-all-time dreams; I mean weird and crazy. I have woken up in the morning and wondered how in the world I just dreamed what I dreamed. Have you ever gone back to sleep and tried to finish a dream? It is goofy, but Grandpa has, and I think it worked. In this story I am going to tell you of a dream that I had for five straight nights. I was a senior in high school, and it was Homecoming Week. We had a good football team and were undefeated. I can't remember for sure, but I don't think our defense had been scored on, or we had only allowed a few points. Homecoming Week was always exciting in Evart. The school and the downtown stores made it a big deal. There was always a parade where the team sat on a hay wagon. Evart Wildcats were going to play the Farwell Eagles on the next Saturday afternoon. I really enjoyed playing in front of a wild, boisterous crowd, and that's always what happened at the Homecoming game.

It was during Homecoming Week when I began to have my dream. Farwell had one of the best running backs in the league. He was big, fast, and strong. He weighed around 210 pounds. That is a big running back for high school football. I had the adrenaline flowing throughout the week, knowing that I would need to tackle that big boy many times. This dream happened in the middle of the night on Monday. This running back took a delayed handoff from his quarterback. What I mean by that is that the quarterback went back like he was going to pass, and the running back looked like he was going to block. Then the quarterback would hand off to the running back, hoping that the defense had spread out looking for a pass. Grandkids, remember I was still in the middle of my dream. This big running back took the handoff and was running full speed. I saw what was happening, and I, too, was running at full speed. His 210 pounds and my 185 pounds were going to collide helmet-to-helmet, violently, at the fifty-yard line. At the point just before the helmet-to-helmet collision, I would wake up. With no exaggeration or embellishment, I can truthfully tell you that this dream occurred five straight nights, and I woke up just before we hit head-on. This happened Monday night, Tuesday night, Wednesday night, Thursday night, and Friday night with the same exact dream and waking up in the middle of the night. Grandkids, I know that that is pretty crazy, but it actually happened. I have never had this type of experience before or since. Now let's fast forward to Saturday afternoon. The team was prepared to play, and the stands were filled with many loud and supportive fans. I don't remember the temperature, but it was a nice sunny day. You never wanted inclement weather for Homecoming with all the festivities. I am quite sure this occurred in the third or fourth quarter. Farwell's quarterback was good, and he was passing often. Then it happened. He went back to pass, and there was that big running back blocking. The quarterback did a great job of faking the draw play and then slipped the ball to the running back. I knew exactly what was happening. I had previewed this play on five consecutive nights in my dreams, but this was no dream. Both of us were running full blast at each other like two battering rams. Right at the fifty-yard line in front of all the fans in the stands, my blue and gold Michigan winged helmet rammed into his purple helmet. Fortunately for me, he ended up on his back, and I made the tackle. Everything on this play was precisely like my dream, up to our head-on collision. After I made this tackle, the Evart fans went crazy. Evart went on to win this game forty-seven to thirty-one.

I have thought about those dreams and that tackle many times and still I am confused. I have no idea why I had those crazy dreams for five nights and then it all happened like my dream. Crazy!

I do know that God does use dreams occasionally. There was a woman who lived near Arthurdale, West Virginia. She and her husband were searching for God but were ignorant about how to get saved. She had a dream that a certain man was coming to their house, and that he would lead them to Christ. A short time after her dream, she and her husband heard a knock at their door. There stood the same man who was in her dream. Your great-grandpa Kretoski had the privilege of leading that couple to Jesus. God had prepared their hearts by speaking to her in a dream. Grandkids, that is actually an awesome story. God will use any means possible to bring lost souls to a place of forgiveness and relationship with Christ. Hopefully, God will use you many times to lead sinners to Jesus. There goes Grandpa's mind again. We just went from football to soul winning.

> "And it shall come to pass afterward, that I will pour out my Spirit upon all flesh; and your sons and your daughters shall prophesy, your old men shall dream dreams, your young men shall see visions:"
>
> JOEL 2:38 (KJV)

SUICIDE SQUEEZE

We moved to Evart in the late summer of 1969. I was going into ninth grade and loved football. Your great-grandpa was a superb athlete, and he wanted his only son, Grandpa, to be good, also. Great-Grandpa told me he was the starting quarterback on varsity, when he was a freshman in high school. I have seen parents try to drive their children to get better. They just push and push. Your great-grandpa never did that, nor did he have to. I was self-motivated. Nobody forced me to play, to lift weights, to attend practice, or to run five miles a day for two weeks to get prepared for football. I did not want to collapse in August when we started practicing twice a day. (I only did that as a senior.) Grandkids, if you really want to excel in an area, be self-motivated. Your parents should never have to push you or nag you to get better. At any rate, Great-Grandpa always admonished me never to put sports in front of Jesus. Actually that is an easy thing to do concerning anything in life—whether it is sports, electronics, or something else.

I can remember my very first day of football practice at Evart. I was the new kid and did not know any of the coaches or players except for a few Pineview boys who played football. Grandkids, guess what that great-grandpa of yours did? He marched into the coaches' office after practice and introduced himself to several coaches. I had no idea he was doing this. I would have been mortified. He told them that Joey Kretoski was his son and that he did not want football to interfere with church attendance or other church activities. This applied not only to his son but also for the Pineview boys. He was their pastor. Wow! I loved my dad, but I was relieved to see your great-grandpa walk out of the locker room that day. The head football coach at Evart was a rather volatile man and a screamer, and most of the players were intimidated by him. I must say, though, that this man probably taught me more fundamentals in football and baseball than any coach I ever had. He was loud and wild, but he was smart. Underneath that harsh façade was a man who deeply cared for his players. He just wanted his players to be the best that they could be and to win. Your grandpa did not like to be screamed at.

At this time I was in ninth grade, and we were still in our two-a-day practices. School had not started, so we practiced in the morning and the late afternoon. The coaches taught many fundamentals during this time, but the practices were normally two hours long and were grueling. They wanted us to be in good shape, and they worked our tails off. When I was in tenth grade, we ended every two-a-day practice with the MSU conditioning drill, which consisted of many, many sprints. This consisted of the whole football team lining up on the goal line after a very arduous practice. We were hot and already exhausted, and we had to run the sprints with our full uniform on, which included our helmets. We had to run fifty-five sprints! We started with ten ten-yard sprints and then did nine twenty-yard sprints. We worked our way down to one one-hundred-yard sprint. It was hard, but I was in the best shape of my life. On this day, we were near the end of a practice, and all of the players from varsity, junior varsity, and the ninth-grade team were in the same area. I don't remember what I said or did, but the head coach started screaming at me in front of everyone. I was slightly embarrassed, but mostly angry. I could feel the blood rush to my head. Here was the most feared adult at Evart High School yelling at me. I raised my hand and interrupted him, saying, "You don't have to scream at me. I can understand you when you just talk to me." It got very, very quiet as every coach and player expected the head coach to explode and go nuts on me, but just the opposite occurred. He did not scream and go "haywire" but talked to me rationally. He still screamed at the other players, but he never even raised his voice to me. We had a mutual respect for each other that continued as long as he coached, and we actually became friends. In fact, my dad took him out fishing and talked to him about being saved. This is the same coach who sent me a congratulatory card for achieving honorable mention all-state during my junior year in football.

This coach was also our baseball coach. We normally had to start baseball practice in the gym because of Michigan's snowy spring weather. He would teach us baseball fundamentals from A to Z. We would hit baseballs off a tube into the dividing curtain. Step into the ball, keep your head on the ball, keep your swing level, and follow through properly. We hit many balls into the curtain and developed our hitting skills. We would play pepper, then he taught us how to steal bases, etc. The coach's favorite time was near the end of practice. He would line us up in the Evart basketball gymnasium and hit wicked grounders and one-hop-line drives at us. We had to keep our heads down on the ball. We had to stop a bad bounce with our body and couldn't let the ball get by us. He had better see the top of our heads when that ball hit our glove, and we had better have that glove on the floor. I have seen this man hit the ball too high, and it would hit the wall and put dents in it. Is it any wonder that I never had a ball go under my glove or through my legs during my senior year? I made throwing errors playing third base, but the ball did not get past me.

I remember a game against Chippewa Hills when I was in tenth grade. We were playing at the old Barryton ballfield. I got up to bat with the bases loaded. Grandkids, the third-base coach is normally the head coach. If you ever watch a third-base coach, he will get rather involved when giving signs to the batter and the runners. He will touch his arms, face, elbows, bill of his cap, etc. Each touching point is a sign of what the coach wants you to do. Does he want you not to swing at the next pitch, is the hit run on, bunt, suicide squeeze, or just hit away? If my memory serves me correctly, after the coach touched his belt, the very next sign was what he wanted you to do. Now the bases were loaded, and I thought the coach gave me the suicide squeeze sign. What this means is that the runner on third base is running to home plate during the pitch. The batter needs to bunt the ball to allow the runner to score. If you miss the pitch and don't bunt, the runner is tagged out easily. Here came the pitch. It was a high and outside fastball. I was trying to bunt, but the pitch was so far out of the strike zone that I could not bunt, but I sure embarrassed myself trying. The umpire called a strike, and no runner came in from third. There stood the coach just shaking his head at me and wondering what in the world I was doing. I had misread his sign. Before the next pitch he did not give me any signs. He just looked at me sarcastically and said, "Hit away." I tried to refocus and waited for the next pitch. Another fastball that was hittable. I swung and hit a long line drive that got past the outfielders. I can still remember sliding into third base and looking up into the coach's face. I had a gigantic smile on my face, and the coach just looked at me and said, "You Polack." I can remember it like it was yesterday. We ended up winning that game, I think, ten to six. I actually hit a three-run-homer, also. I ended up with six RBIs.

There will be times in life when we embarrass ourselves. It is going to happen unless you are a reclusive hermit. Be embarrassed, feel stupid for a while, learn from it, and then move on. Allow yourself to grow as a person. I looked like a complete idiot when I tried to bunt that ball. I would assume that players were snickering in both dugouts. I would have laughed at that type of mistake. Just refocus and try not to take yourself too seriously. Don't be afraid to laugh at yourself. I have done it zillions of times.

Grandkids, you will also come in contact with abrasive and perhaps potentially intimidating people, just like my coach. I am not saying that you need to replicate what Grandpa did, but never cower to another person, even a person in authority. Respect them, but don't ever cower and be fearful. Your great-grandma used to tell me that they are just people. Always stand up for what is right. We lead by doing, but there may be times when you have to speak out against an unfair situation. Be strong and respectful.

"Have I not commanded you? Be strong and courageous. Do not be frightened, and do not be dismayed, for the Lord your God is with you wherever you go."

JOSHUA 1:9 (ESV)

Marijuana Brownie

It is incredible how many people use drugs and drink alcohol. Even when I was in high school, drugs and alcohol were routinely used by many students, including some of my friends. I have counseled many kids over the years who have struggled with drugs and alcohol. Oftentimes, it was a generational situation. Their grandparents and parents struggled, also. I do believe that many of the kids I counseled were using drugs to help them cope with their pain and their dysfunctional situations. Grandkids, once you start, it is extremely hard to stop—not just drugs and alcohol but anything addictive. Listen up! Don't take the first drink, don't "pop" the first pill, and don't take the first puff, and you will never have to struggle with stopping. An ounce of prevention is worth a pound of cure!

When I pastored in Elkins, West Virginia, I would customarily visit in the community on Sunday afternoons. I would just go for a walk and be neighborly. On this afternoon I decided to visit a brother of one of our church members. I knocked on his door, and when he opened the door my olfactory glands were assaulted with this pukey, sweet aroma. There were five guys in the living room, and they were smoking weed. I just walked in and played ignorant. I chitchatted for a while as I watched the smoke spiral from behind their backs. I then had to vacate. That smell and THC was getting to my head. Before I left, though, I asked the brother if I could pray with them, and he graciously consented. He probably just wanted me out of his house. Anyway, I bowed my head and began to thank God for sending His Son to earth so that mankind could find deliverance. Then I prayed that those five men in that room would find Jesus and forgiveness for sins. I stank like a "pothead" when I left that house but was thankful for the opportunity to witness. I was very kind and respectful to those men. It was not my job to condemn them and to be harsh, but to share Jesus.

Another time I was on a school bus traveling back from a baseball game with the team. I was a senior in high school. They were passing a two-liter Coke around, and when it came in front of me, I took a swig of it. I immediately felt the burn of the alcohol and spat it out. Some of the players weren't too happy that I gave them a sticky shower when I did. One of the players had mixed together rum and Coke in a Coke bottle, and I had innocently begun to drink it. I had never even tasted alcohol before but instantly knew it contained some. Let me qualify that statement. Your wonderful and saintly great-grandpa Kretoski gave me beer in my bottle when I was just beginning to walk and thought it was funny when I could not keep my equilibrium. Great-Grandma was furious. He had not gotten saved yet and really did not understand the seriousness of his actions or its sinfulness. Grandkids, when someone truly finds Christ, it will change them inwardly and outwardly. I did not make a big deal out of the rum-and-coke situation. The coach was oblivious to everything. Some of the players were shocked that I even took a drink, because they knew I was a Christian. I surely was shocked after I took the drink.

A person can easily become dependent on illegal or legal drugs. I am going to tell you a personal story of how Grandpa grew dependent on a legal drug. When I was in my middle fifties, I was experiencing severe pain in both my knees. My left knee was bone-on-bone with minimal ligament support. The right knee just hurt many times with a severe, red-hot pain. I had received several cortisone shots and even gel-lubricating shots. These shots were excruciating as the doctor would penetrate the skin and then push that needle in behind my kneecap and release the medicinal fluid into my knee. One time I jerked so badly that the doctor stabbed himself with my needle. I told him to be happy that I did not have AIDS. He wasn't overly happy with my sarcasm. It was during one of those visits that this caring doctor questioned me as to whether my knee pain affected my sleep. Yes, it did. There were nights when I found it difficult to go to sleep and then stay asleep because of the discomfort. He asked me if I wanted something to help me to sleep. I trusted my doctor and told him "yes" with only a slight reservation. I began to take ten milligrams of Ambien just before bedtime. I would read in bed for a while and then fall asleep rather easily. I noticed that when I had the left knee replaced, and the right knee's pain seemed to lesson, I still needed that little white pill to sleep. After a few years, I questioned my primary care doctor on the side effects of Ambien, and he assured me of its medicinal benefits. He had taken it for thirty years with no ill effects, and he even prescribed it for his own mother. My mind was pacified again, and I trusted my doctor. I would hear tidbits of negativity concerning sleeping pills but chose to ignore them. I then began to experience some different ill effects. I did not fall asleep so readily at times. Sometimes I would wake up in a fog, and it might take two or three hours for me to feel alert. There was a time when I walked out of a store and was confused as to the whereabouts of my Pathfinder. There were times I could not remember simple things and grew frustrated with myself. I thought my brain was becoming "dementi-ated" (Grandpa's word), or I was in the beginning of Alzheimer's disease.

My sister, Carol, talked to me concerning Ambien. She said it was addictive and had some rather horrible side effects. Grandkids, I can be rather stubborn and narrow-minded at times, but I listened to your Aunt Carol that time. I kept thinking of my debilitating sleep, my fogginess, and my memory loss. I began to research Ambien on the Internet. As I read about the side effects, I was scared and amazed at the same time. It seemed as though I was reading about myself at times. There were many negative side effects, and Grandpa was experiencing some of them. When I read that it could possibly lead to Alzheimer's, I was on high alert. I knew I had to get off this poison. I was as bad off and dependent as any person I had ever counseled. I had used this drug for almost eight years, and it was making my mind goofy. I was then sixty-two years old and tried to stop using Ambien gradually for two or three nights. I cut my pill in half. I read until late, tossed and turned, prayed, did every relaxation exercise known to mankind, and ended up taking the remainder of my Ambien at three-thirty or four in the morning. I had to get a little bit of sleep. It was crazy, but Grandpa was totally hooked on that junk. I continued to take an Ambien every night before bedtime. I was still dependent and knew I needed to stop using it. I was now sixty-three and had a new doctor. She disliked Ambien, and we discussed strategy. We decided that I would take a lesser-evil sleeping pill that potentially had some positive effects. For three straight nights, I took Trazadone as my replacement drug. I am not sure whether it was my reaction to the Trazadone or my withdrawal from Ambien, but things got very weird for your grandpa. My head was spinning, and my balance was bad. I was sitting in the Lazy Boy, and I saw a light shining out of our bedroom. The problem was that there was not a light on; Grandpa was hallucinating. I have never had panic attacks, and I was fighting them off. I felt like my feet were going to explode. When I finally went to bed at four or five in the morning, my legs were aching. It felt like I had severe shin splints as I lay in bed. I would sit in the chair during the day and have tremors. I would only sleep one or two hours during the night. This craziness went on for three straight nights, but I knew I had to break my dependency to Ambien. I was very determined, and the Kretoski stubbornness set in. I was thinking that third morning how bizarre the situation was and decided to go off Trazadone, also. After three nights of misery, I went off all sleeping pills "cold turkey." I was just done with taking those little white pills. I asked Grandma to throw the Ambien away. I realized that I needed more Divine intervention. I requested that several people pray for me, and I drove to our pastor's home. He was outside at the time, and I told him my situation. He laid his hands on me and prayed passionately for me. With God's help and my resolution that I would not take those evil pills, I slowly but surely began to break my dependency. As this story is being written, it has been about three weeks since I went off those pills "cold turkey." I am no longer dependent and have none of those weird side effects. Thank the Lord! My sleeping was somewhat erratic as my mind and body adjusted to being drug-free, but I am free and will remain free through God's help. I am learning to sleep in bed more and more. It is a process and just takes time. Grandkids, my fogginess is beginning to dissipate and hopefully my memory will be fully restored. I still struggle a little, but I think it is all getting better. This experience will surely help Grandpa be more sensitive and caring to others who are struggling with an addiction or a dependency.

I am finally getting to the story about the marijuana brownie. Hang on tightly, because this story gets a little goofy. I was nineteen years old when this story took place, while working at Evart Products. I worked there for over a year before I went to college. I did this for two reasons: one was that I needed to save money for college, and secondly, I wanted to develop a dislike for working in a factory. I accomplished both. I would always pay God's tithe and then put most of the remainder of my check into my savings account. Your grandpa was actually rather frugal. I did not want to lose sight of my goal, which was graduating from college. For a young man, I had one of the best jobs in the shop, which was running the parts warehouse on third shift. I had my own desk, phone, and forklift truck. There were over four thousand parts in that warehouse, and I needed to know where things were. Fortunately, I never had a difficult time memorizing numbers, so I learned this job rather easily. In the beginning it was overwhelming, but you just keep your nose to the grind and, "presto," you've got it. My biggest challenge was to stay awake. My circadian system was set to work during the daylight hours. During a regular shift, a person had two fifteen-minute breaks and a thirty-minute lunch break. It was during one of my breaks that I noticed a pan full of brownies sitting on one of the tables. Anybody could take one. Your old grandpa has a "sweet tooth," so the natural thing to do was to take one, which I did. I took a bite, and it tasted awful. That was the worst-tasting brownie that I had ever tasted! The woman who had baked the brownies was sitting at the table, watching me rather intently. I just thought that she was a terrible cook and did not want to hurt her feelings. These brownies were rather fibrous, but I just kept chewing and swallowing. Finally, I finished the nasty morsel, but the nasty morsel was not finished with me. My head began to spin out of control. I began to walk back to the warehouse. Now my head was not only spinning, but was totally weird. It was kind of like riding a roller coaster at an amusement park. It finally hit me what had occurred. I had eaten a brownie that was mixed with marijuana. Grandkids, remember that grandpa did not drink alcohol or use drugs and had no tolerance for any drugs. I felt like my body was out of control. I was moving very slowly and felt like I was floating. Things got rather fuzzy, and there I was driving a forklift, which was stupid and dangerous. I finally realized what I needed to do. I went to my foreman and told him I was sick and needed to go home. If he was observant he probably would have noticed my pupils were dilated as big as nickels. This was the only time I missed work in this fifteen-month period before I went to college. Now how in the world does a person drive home when his mind is totally buzzed? It was not easy, but fortunately, there was no traffic, since it was in the middle of the night. I rolled my window down, stuck my head out of the window, and began to slowly drive to Pineview. I parked my car, walked in Barton House, and went to bed. I don't remember anything about how I slept, but I do remember that when I woke up my head felt like a big melon. I have had numerous people tell me that you don't experience a hangover from pot, but I definitely did. I felt weird for several hours and then got ready for work. The more I thought about the situation, the more frustrated and angry I became. There were two people who I knew about who were involved with those brownies—the woman whom I assumed baked them and her male friend. During my shift, this man walked through the warehouse. This wasn't very Christian, but I grabbed him by the front of his shirt, slammed him against some crates, and began to question him. He began to apologize profusely and told me they were shocked that I took a brownie. They knew I was a Christian and wanted to stop me but were fearful that they would get themselves in trouble. I had attended school with this guy, and I think he had actually attended my dad's church at least once. His sister was a regular attendee. So they chose to be silent, the sissies! He begged me not to tell my foreman and continued to apologize. He knew he would lose his job and possibly have a date with the police. I finally let his feet hit terra firma, and he returned to his workstation as a rather anxious young man. I was very thankful that nothing tragic happened the night before while I was working and then driving home.

I have thought of this situation many times over the years. When I was high, I felt like my world was out of control. Everything was unbalanced and whacked out. Grandkids, why would anyone purposefully drink, smoke, snort, ingest, or inject themselves with a substance that can drastically alter their mind and even their body? I recently visited a woman in the hospital who had abused prescription drugs and illegal drugs for many years. She looked at least twenty years older than she actually was. I prayed for her and her family, and tried to lead them to Jesus. It is a very challenging thing to overcome an addiction or a dependency. The body just craves that substance, and the person thinks he can't live without it. Grandpa once counseled a man who was addicted to crack cocaine for many years. He was raised by Christian parents but made poor choices. His life was horribly out of control, and he was blessed to be alive. I'm going to make a long story short. He gave his life to Jesus, had a loving pastor, had some relapses, but eventually got clean, and stayed clean. Every time I see this guy, I ask him if his pupils are constricted. He has served God and turned his life totally around. Most are not this fortunate.

Grandkids, I have said this before and will probably say it again, "Don't start, and you will never have to stop." Also, if you ever begin to eat a brownie that tastes nasty, throw it away immediately!

"Don't be drunk with wine, because that will ruin your life. Instead, be filled with the Holy Spirit."

EPHESIANS 5:18 (NLT)

It's Not Fair

When the weather warmed up in the spring, your grandpa was consumed by baseball. I loved to play the game, I loved the Pittsburgh Pirates, and I loved Roberto Clemente. He was the right-fielder for the Pirates and a great hitter. He was my all-time favorite baseball player. My little league coach taught us to catch a fly ball with two hands. He hollered at me often as I would make a classic Clemente basket catch. I rarely dropped a ball so he wasn't too hard on me. He actually just wanted me to be a good leader for the other players.

Fairmont was a town of approximately twenty thousand people, and its little league program was a big deal. Fairmont was actually in the Little League World Series back in the fifties, and I think the prominence of the game was a carryover of its glory days. There was always a box score in the Fairmont paper, and there were times when the paper would actually write articles concerning Little League. I remember an article in the paper about a Little League player who finally lost a game as a pitcher. This pitcher had won over twenty straight games, and it was a rare occasion when he actually lost a game, three to two. Grandpa rather enjoyed that story, because I was that winning pitcher. That kid only lost one game in his little league career.

Many times in the summer I would ride my bike to Twelfth Street Stadium in the late morning. It was several miles from my house. I would then weasel myself under the large gate and then drag my bike under the

175

gate, also. I would play baseball with several other boys who had also sneaked into the stadium. Many times I would play until late afternoon. Yes, Grandkids, I would even miss my lunch. There would be times when I would rush home to grab a bite to eat, put on my uniform, and ride all the way back to play a real game that evening. I never grew tired of playing baseball or making my Roberto Clemente basket catch.

Grandpa loved to hit and run the bases, but I was also the team's main pitcher. Now back in the day, ole grandpa had a wicked fastball, but I did have one major problem. Grandpa was wild. What that means is that there were times when Grandpa had trouble throwing strikes. Opposing batters had a rough time getting settled into the batter's box. They were afraid that I would unleash a wild pitch and hit them with a sizzling fastball. There was one game when Grandpa walked eighteen batters. Yes, Grandkids, I did say eighteen. I think I also hit three or four batters with wild pitches. That has to be some type of record for one pitcher. I also struck out sixteen batters that game. I remember this game rather distinctly because I became so frustrated with the umpire. He kept calling pitches balls that I thought were strikes. You could tell when I got really upset when pitching, because I got really wild. There were a few times when I threw the ball totally over everybody's head. The ball would hit the back of the backstop. My coach, Mr. Bunner, was very patient with me. He would try to get me to focus and would always encourage me. What is crazy about this game is that I won the game. I walked eighteen, struck out sixteen, and only gave up one hit. The final score was nine to eight.

The Little League regular season finally came to an end. Now it was time for the all-star games. I am assuming that the coaches got together and decided who would be on the all-star team. I was rather certain that I would be one of the representatives for my team, the Kiwanis. I was relieved and very happy when it was announced that I was an all-star. A dream had come true. I was an American League All-Star. It was during this time when my family made a trip to Michigan to attend the United Holiness church camp. We were there for several days and returned to West Virginia. I knew that I had missed one all-star practice but rationalized that the head coach would understand. I really did not have a choice but to go to Michigan. I still remember going to the next scheduled practice. I went full of expectations and energy. I got to the practice, and the coach looked at me and said that I was no longer on the team. I tried to explain to him what had happened but his mind was made up. He was coldhearted and so blunt. My coach was at that practice. I don't remember if he was an assistant coach or what. I went and talked with him and told him my situation. He was very upset and went over to the head coach. I could hear them arguing and was hoping that the head coach would listen. Then my coach lost his temper and called that man every nasty name known unto mankind. I just stood there with a broken heart. I knew my chance of playing on the all-star team was lost. It was one of the worst times of Grandpa's life. I was truly dejected and discouraged.

It took Grandpa several days to deal with this depressing situation, but I eventually rolled with the punches and returned my attention to football. I have thought of this situation dozens of times over the years. I have come to the conclusion that this man was being vengeful. Grandkids, do you remember the pitcher who lost only one game in his little league career? This was his father and coach. I think he was being totally vindictive and mean. He also did not want me to steal any of the limelight from his son, who was also an all-star. I remember listening to the all-star games on the radio and so longingly wanted to hear the announcer use my name. I knew I deserved to be there. I'm sixty-three years old as I write this story, and there is still a small part of my heart that hurts.

Grandkids, if I have said it once, I have said it a dozen times. Life is not always fair. There will probably be times when you will be treated unfairly or even with nastiness. With God's help, you can move past that situation in time—at least mostly past it. Have I forgiven that cruel all-star coach? Of course! It just took time—maybe a long time. Would it have been wonderful to play in the all-star games? Most definitely, but this was just a small fragment of my life. I still played six more years of baseball. I started on varsity in high school for three years as a third baseman. Then after high school I played on several softball teams. Life is good, and I hope that I meet that mean, nasty coach in Heaven.

"And we know that for those who love God all things work together for good, for those who are called according to His purpose."

ROMANS 8:28 (ESV)

"Be not overcome of evil, but overcome evil with good."

ROMAN 12:21 (KJV)

MURDERER

This next story is about when Grandpa received his first gun. My father, your great-grandpa, truly enjoyed to hunt and fish. He actually enjoyed most sports and was an excellent athlete. My dad was the best horseshoe pitcher I ever saw. When we moved back to West Virginia in the fall of 1963, Great-Grandpa was anxious to hunt and fish again. He did fish a time or two in the Sierra Nevada Mountains. I remember when he fished in those mountains with his brother, and they caught many native trout. There was a problem, though. I think Great-Grandpa told me that they killed eighteen rattlesnakes and had a wild bull ram his Plymouth station wagon. He said it was very hard to enjoy their fishing with so many rattlesnakes. Many times when one snake was detected, they would find another one in close proximity. Great-Grandpa was happy to be back in his beloved West Virginia mountains. He did not always take me squirrel hunting with him. Great-Grandpa would normally still hunt for squirrels. This means that he would stealthily sneak through the woods by moving a short distance and then pausing for some time. He would sit at times if he found a productive hickory grove but preferred to stalk squirrels. This is probably why he did not take me squirrel hunting much. I would make too much noise. Now, Grandkids, when it came to rabbit hunting, I rarely got left at home. We did not have a good rabbit dog yet, so Grandpa became the dog. I jumped on every brush pile and stomped through every briar patch. The green running briars in West Virginia are terrible to walk through. They rip your clothing and your body. My legs, arms, and even my face got scratched up, but I never complained. I loved rabbit hunting. I did have one longing, though, and that was to have my own gun. I was only eight, but it just did not seem right for me not to be carrying a gun. I would spend many nights looking through the Sears catalog and just dream of owning one of the many shotguns that were displayed. I will discuss at the end of this story how I received my first gun. Just hold on, and be patient.

The next fall I had my new gun and began squirrel hunting more with Great-Grandpa. We would get up early on a Saturday morning. I was a heavy sleeper, and Great-Grandma would have to wake me up several times every morning for school. However, when we were to go squirrel hunting, Great-Grandpa told me that he would wake me up once and that I needed to get up promptly. Grandkids, do you know what would have happened if I had not gotten up? Great-Grandpa would have left me. This was actually really good for Grandpa, because it forced me to discipline myself. I always got up; I loved to be with my dad and to hunt. We would enter the woods when it was dark, and Great-Grandpa would take me near a den tree or where he knew some squirrels were likely to be. I was nine years old, and Great-Grandpa did not take me with him but left me next to a tree on some steep mountainside. Great-Grandpa always prayed for squirrels and protection before we went into the woods. He told me he would be back in an hour or two, and he left me. Grandkids, I was only nine, and my imagination was going berserk. I was thinking about copperheads and bears. The woods are actually full of noise if a person is quiet and grows acclimated to the environment. That morning every noise was a predator coming after me. I knew that Great-Grandpa told me that God would protect me and that I did not have to worry, but my faith was puny. It eventually grew light, and some of my anxiety dissipated, but I was still alone in the big bad woods.

Grandkids, let me take you down another bunny trail for a minute. These figures can vary, but probably ninety-five percent of anxiety is imagined and about five percent is real. Sometimes we allow our minds to go crazy about what might happen but rarely does happen. The problem is that oftentimes we don't overcome this imaginary anxiety, and it plagues us as adults. Be careful in this area, and place your trust in Jesus.

Now back to the story. Guess what? Great-Grandpa always came back. I would hear him shoot a few times, and he would normally come back with a few squirrels in his game pouch. I never shot a squirrel my first few times hunting. I probably made too much noise. You might be wondering why Great-Grandpa Kretoski left me in the woods by myself at such a young age. That's just how Great-Grandpa was. I'm assuming he wanted his son to be strong and manly. When he was eight and nine years old, he was "running" moonshine, fishing all night, and stealing coal off the trains by himself. He probably never thought about his son becoming fearful and anxious. This forced me to be strong and trusting. It made me a better person who did not always cater to my emotions. We just can't allow our emotions to dictate our behavior all the time.

I remember hunting with your great-grandpa while I was in high school. On this day my gun was a Remington sixteen-gauge pump. It held five shells. We had been hunting all morning long, and I was tired. We ate some salami sandwiches and probably some boiled eggs for lunch, and then went back out hunting. The sun was shining, and it was a warm fall day. I sat down and put my back up against a log and fell soundly asleep. I don't know how long I slept, but I was awakened from my sleep very abruptly. Somebody shot very close to me. Then I heard a flop next to me. A squirrel had almost landed on top of me. There stood your great-grandpa with one of the biggest smiles known unto mankind, and then he just started laughing. He had just shot a squirrel out of a tree directly above my head. What a memory!

Another time we were hunting squirrels on Mr. Parson's property. Mr. Parson's woods was across the road from the parsonage. Dad and I were walking on the edge of the property when a fox squirrel jumped up on a large tree about one hundred feet from us. Great-Grandpa told me to sneak around that tree and shoot that squirrel. I sneakily walked to that tree and very quietly began to sneak to the other side. Your great-grandpa was a trickster. He knew that when I stalked that squirrel around that tree that it would slide to the other side and give him an easy shot. One more time I heard a *ka-boom*. He shot, and there was another dead squirrel. He just stood there smiling and began to laugh again. He then told me the proper procedure. If you see a squirrel jump on a tree and hide on the opposite side, get a stick and throw it on the other side of the tree, and it will cause the squirrel to slide around for an easy shot. It works. I have done it several times.

Now back to the story of my first gun. It was October, and squirrel and rabbit seasons were quickly approaching. I remember Great-Grandpa telling Great-Grandma that he was going to buy me a gun for an early Christmas gift. Grandkids, your great-grandma was one of the finest women who ever was born. She was kind, empathic, funny, hardworking, loving, but could also be quite frank. She and Great-Grandpa had a very strong marriage, and they loved and respected each other. They did not always agree, but I couldn't ever remember them lashing out at each other. That was about to change. When Great-Grandma realized that Great-Grandpa was actually going to purchase a gun for me, she was not a happy camper. It was at this point where Great-Grandma called Great-Grandpa a murderer several times rather emotionally. Her motives were pure, but she was very reactionary. She just loved her sweet and innocent little boy. I can't really remember Great-Grandpa's response, but he did not just stand there and argue. Great-Grandpa thought he was right and that I was mature enough to be responsible with a gun. We got into the car and drove a rather long distance to a gun store. There were racks of guns. I thought I had died and gone to Heaven. This store was a thousand times better than the Sears catalog, and I was mesmerized. Great-Grandpa found the gun that he was looking for and handed it to me. It was a Stevens single shot youth model twenty-gauge. It was the prettiest gun I had ever seen or handled. This was the perfect gun for me, and I adored it. I could not believe that now I owned my own gun. My dream had come true. I have owned many guns over the years, but none have ever meant as much as my first gun. Someday I am going to will it to one of my grandkids.

I did eventually shoot my share of rabbits and squirrels with that twenty-gauge. Your great-grandpa was an excellent shot with a shotgun and rarely missed, while your grandpa was another matter. I missed a lot of rabbits and squirrels but surely had fun.

"Now then, take your weapons, your quiver and your bow, and go out to the field and hunt game for me."

GENESIS 27:3 (ESV)

FIRE AND BRIMSTONE

Well, Grandkids, this title probably got your attention. This story took place at a camp meeting while Grandpa was in high school and is the total opposite of the previous stories I have written about camp-meeting experiences. In those stories I was the bad guy being chased by camp cops, but in this particular story, I was a camp cop along with two of my friends, Danny and Greg. You may wonder how in the world a teenager could become a camp cop. I don't remember to whom I talked, but I essentially just told the person that we were going to be cops that year. I thought that he would laugh at me, just say "no," or tell me that I was crazy. I can't imagine a teenager coming up to me as an adult and telling me that he and two of his friends were planning on taking over the camp cop positions. Grandpa would probably just laugh and ask the teenager if his pupils were dilated. Anyway, there was no conflict about us doing the cop job. I don't remember how Greg and Danny reacted, but I was rather flabbergasted. Somebody in authority probably should have just been strong and said "no," but instead allowed a strong-willed teenage boy to manipulate the system. I would actually have accepted and respected a negative response, because that is exactly what I expected.

Grandkids, when you grow up to be an adult, be strong, and when needed, be decisive. Don't ever look down on people because of your age or position. I have seen many people grow arrogant and develop a superior attitude, because they received some authority or power due to their position in life. I remember a time when I was a senior in high school, and we had a meeting with an administrator concerning graduation. I never particularly liked this certain man. He just acted like he was better or superior to others, and I never appreciated that in any person, but I always treated him with respect. In this particular meeting, which was attended by the whole senior class, he went into his loud and disrespectful mode and embarrassed a couple of girls. He continued to display his arrogant attitude by just being "snippy" and disrespectful to students. In retrospect, Grandpa probably should have "superglued" his lips, but I made a negative comment to him concerning his disrespectful attitude. He reacted with anger and kicked me out of the meeting. I did not verbally respond to his loud directive but just walked out of the meeting. When I went to close the door to the classroom, I was in for a shock. Probably half the boys in the senior class walked out with me, and it was not a good situation. Now, as an adult and authority figure, the administrator should have called me into his office to discuss this nasty situation. We needed to process and be reconciled. He never spoke to me again and totally ignored me for the remainder of the school year. This scenario was actually quite sad and should never have happened. He should have been respectful and patient, and I should have been more respectful. Grandkids, it is so easy to "spout off" when you are irritated. Remember Proverbs 15:1, "A gentle answer turns away anger, but a harsh word stirs up anger." (NIV) Always try to rise above negative people, and never fall to their level. It does not matter what others do; always remain respectful and kind. As Christians we overcome evil with good. This is a real challenge, but it is the right thing to do. Grandpa has had to apologize to some people over the years because of his negative responses. I am sixty-three years old as I write this story, and there are still times when I find it very difficult not to respond to another's negativity.

Now to get back to my original story. We actually were very responsible, and camp went well. It was kind of funny when we would disguise our voices and tell older people that they needed to quiet down a little. We would walk away from their campers and just laugh. Now on this particular night we were doing our rounds on the grounds and were checking out the dining hall. We walked back to the cooking area and saw some freshly baked bread and noticed there was some sliced roast beef in the large refrigerator. We each took a chunk of the loaf of home-made bread and some roast beef and had a midnight snack. We really did not think about this situation very thoroughly, but allowed our salivary longings to overwhelm our common sense. We finally finished our rounds and went to sleep with full bellies. The next morning we went to the youth service a little late, and the speaker that morning was also the camp cook. I have never heard a person speak with such anger. He was extremely upset that someone had the audacity to steal his bread and roast beef. Those thieves were going to be thrown into a pit of fire and brimstone at the Judgment. We sat there very quietly and would not make eye contact with each other or the speaker. He was so angry that he was almost frothing at the mouth. We were relieved when he finally dismissed the service, and we were able to get away from his righteous indignation. I don't blame him for being angry and irritated, but he sure expressed his anger in an unholy manner. Years later this man and his family visited our church on missionary deputation, and they came to our home for dinner. Yes, Grandkids, I told him exactly what happened and apologized to him. I did explain to him that we were really not intentionally stealing but did make a bad choice. I think I re-aggravated him, and he did not seem too pleased with my confession. Life goes on.

Grandkids, just try to think before you act, and always try to treat others as you would want to be treated.

"There is one who speaks rashly like the thrusts of a sword, but the tongue of the wise brings healing."

PROVERBS 12:18 (NASB)

Searching
(Grandma's Testimony)

When I (Grandma) was eighteen years old, my life was gloriously changed. Sunday school and church in the small rural village of Chippewa Lake, Michigan, had been a part of my life as long as I could remember. By the time I was eighteen, I had been awarded pins by our Sunday school to prove that I had had perfect attendance for ten years in a row. Assisting with Vacation Bible School, participating in Christmas programs and Easter sunrise services, serving at church meals, singing in the choir—these were all part of my growing-up years. Unfortunately, I don't ever remember hearing the plan of salvation there, but perhaps it was because Satan had deafened my ears to hearing the Gospel. So, in spite of being very involved in church, I still felt a great void in my life that I had no idea how to fill. I loved singing the hymns and hearing the church chimes ring out songs such as "The Old Rugged Cross" over the lake and throughout the community on Sunday mornings. There are still many hymns we sing that often remind me of that little church on the hill—the same church that some of my great-grandparents and grandparents attended before me.

From the time I was a small child, insecurity was an issue that constantly plagued me. Being extremely shy made it very difficult for me to speak up in school, except when a teacher called on me to answer a question. Fortunately, God gifted me with the ability to do well in school, so I did enjoy learning and the academic part of school. Because of this, I eventually graduated in 1972 as the salutatorian of my graduating class of 161 students. However, I was never athletic, at least as far as school sports went. Loving to swim, I did take swimming lessons for several years. The year that I took Junior Lifesaving, I was too young to receive a certificate and never went back to get it, since I felt like I knew enough about saving someone if needed. I also loved to roller-skate and spent many summer afternoons and evenings at our local roller rink. But in school sports at P.E. time, I was very deficient. I know how it feels to be the last or one of the last ones chosen to be on a team. I'll never forget the devastating feeling that came every time it happened and do hope that teachers have figured out a better way to choose teams by now! Those experiences only contributed to my feelings of insecurity.

For others looking on, I suppose it looked like I had it all together. In seventh grade I was elected class president and held some kind of class office every year until I graduated. I could never really figure out why, because I certainly didn't display any leadership ability. It was petrifying to stand up and speak in front of people, and I was constantly being told to speak louder, because no one could hear me. In tenth grade I took a step of courage and registered to take a speech class. The intended purpose was to build my confidence and make it easier for me to speak in front of others. However, I found I was just as far out of my comfort zone giving a speech at the end of the year as at the beginning. Perhaps because others knew I was at the top of my class, they assumed I would be a good class officer.

Involvement in many activities during high school kept me very busy. Attending football and basketball games were always a high priority. Participation in National Honor Society and French Club, working in the school office, dances and proms, being a senior homecoming queen candidate, and frequent dates were all parts of my life. Sewing was also a favorite hobby, and I made most of my own clothes. As I mentioned before, it probably appeared that I had it all together. However, no one knew what was really going on in my heart.

When I became a senior, some of my friends and I started to become involved in drinking and partying. I remember at one football game going out to someone's car and sharing a bottle of wine with my friends. At that time in my life, the legal drinking age was eighteen, but I was only sixteen or seventeen. Other times, we would go to bars. Once I tried to sneak into a bar, using my friend's driver's license, but the person checking the identifications at the door refused to let me in, once he figured out it wasn't my license. So my friends and I just went to another bar where they didn't check the identifications so carefully. I really didn't care about the drinking, but I did love to dance, and those places always had live bands and great dance floors. At any rate, I did start going to lots of parties where things were happening that shouldn't have been. This intensified as I graduated from high school and began attending college at Ferris State in Big Rapids, Michigan, where I earned an associate's degree in dental assisting. Throughout my first year of college, I attended fraternity parties and other events, and tried to fit in with the crowd.

During that first year of college, I lived at home with my parents. I remember coming home from parties and thinking to myself, *Is this all there is to life?* Although I didn't realize it at the time, the Lord had slowly been working on me. Going to the college bookstore, I would buy books about different religions and beliefs, many of them having to do with the new-age movement, which was quite popular at that time. In discussions with friends, I can still hear myself saying, "It doesn't matter what you believe as long as you are sincere." How Satan had me blinded! He must have loved hearing me say that. Thankfully, the Lord continued to deal with me. I had a Bible that had been given to me by my Sunday school, although I don't remember ever reading it. Somehow a modern paraphrase of the Bible came into my possession, although I don't remember reading that too much, either. However, I started reciting the Lord's Prayer every day. This was something I was well-acquainted with because we said it together every Sunday in church. At any rate, God had put a longing in my heart for something beyond myself, and He would soon fulfill that longing.

After graduation from high school, one of my former party friends moved back to Oklahoma to live with her dad and stepmom. We hadn't really kept in contact too much, but the summer after my first year of college, she decided to move back to the area to be close to her mom and stepdad and to attend Ferris. She also wondered if I would like to move into a dorm with her, so we could be roommates. Of course, I told her I would, not knowing that the Lord had radically changed her life. She gradually began witnessing to me, telling me how her life was so different now. Before the school year started, she needed to go back to Oklahoma to get her car and some other things, so she asked me to take the train there with her. We had a great trip, and I enjoyed seeing the different country and meeting the rest of her family. When it was time to drive back to Michigan on a Wednesday morning, there were many tornado watches and warnings in the area, so we decided it would be best to wait another day to leave. That night we attended a service in the church where my friend had been attending. That was probably the first time I had ever gone to a church besides where I had grown up. It was totally different than any church service I had ever been in! The music was so lively, and people even clapped in time to the music. Prayer requests were taken, and many people besides the pastor actually prayed out loud all at the same time. People testified to the grace of God in their lives. The pastor preached a message, and when he was finished, he invited the people to come to the altar to pray. I don't remember a single thing he preached about, but I do remember standing there, clenching the pew in front of me, and feeling very strange. The pastor must have sensed my conviction and came back to ask me if I would like to go to the altar and pray. From what I remember, I didn't hesitate at all. Again, I don't remember anything that I said or that anyone else prayed while I was at the altar, but I do know that when I stood up, something completely wonderful had happened. When I walked out of that church that night, I couldn't believe how incredibly beautiful and bright the stars looked. I had always been so wrapped up in my own little world that I really hadn't been too aware of the world around me. God had worked a miracle and totally transformed me into a new creation, just as the Bible says. All things had become new! Many changes came immediately in my life, such as no longer taking the Lord's name in vain or desiring the party life. Other things took longer, but God was very patient with me and still continues to work on me. From the moment I was saved, my desire was to please God, and in all of these years, that desire has never once changed except to grow stronger. He had been so faithful to orchestrate time and circumstances so that I would be in that little church in Shawnee, Oklahoma, on August 29, 1973, with a friend who had been praying for me.

At that point, I was excited to get home to tell my family and friends about Jesus and what He had done in my life. Working at the Ferris library, I witnessed to anyone who would listen, including all the staff and fellow students. The president of the library, who also happened to be our neighbor and attended our church, called me into her office one day to chat, and I told her how I wanted to join the Peace Corps in order to help people. She told me there were many people to help right here in the United States, and that I didn't need to leave the country to help others. Knowing nothing about Bible colleges or missions, I was reaching out for the only organization that I knew about that sounded like something of which I wanted to be a part. I really was very ignorant of spiritual matters, not knowing that the Holy Spirit would lead and guide me.

My friend and I moved into our new home in the dorm, where we witnessed to all of our friends and eventually got some of them to go to church with us. We had found a church in town from the same denomination in which I was saved, and that church became like our second home. We were there every time the church doors were open, which seemed to be almost every night of the week. Involvement in youth and other church activities, as well as practicing with a singing group of which we became a part, kept us very busy. Our group eventually traveled to different places to sing and minister, which is how we ended up singing at Pineview Homes, where I met your grandpa.

Over the years, God has been very faithful to bless me far beyond anything I could have imagined. Yes, there have been difficult times, but God has been especially near through those. He has given me a Christian husband and two beautiful children who have married wonderful, Christian spouses. And He especially blessed me when He gave me you six grandchildren! God even fulfilled my childhood dream of my becoming a teacher, a dream I had given up because I was too insecure to pursue it in college. Dental assisting had been my choice of degree, because it didn't require any classes speaking in front of people. It is still not easy for me to speak in front of others, and I don't understand why God hasn't made it easier, because I have prayed about it hundreds of times. However, each of us is unique, and since God made me that way, I have tried to accept it and attempted to do the best I can, with His help. He has enabled me to be a teacher and secretary in a Christian school for many years, a Sunday school teacher for kindergarteners and all age groups through teens, a Sunday school superintendent in different churches (which included leading the singing), a missions leader, and a pastor's wife, as well as many other roles over the years since I gave my heart to Him.

My prayer for you grandkids is that you will all give your hearts to Jesus while you are very young, and that you will serve Him with your whole hearts. Satan's plan is to keep you from that, but you will never be truly happy unless you do. We serve such a creative God who has made everyone unique, and desires each of us to use the talents He has given us to glorify Him. Has God given you a goal or dream for your life? He *is* the Dream-Giver. Life becomes so much more meaningful when you have a goal or a dream. While I had always wanted to be a teacher when I was young and didn't think I could do it, you kids have a great advantage over what I had. I had no idea that God wanted to fulfill my dream and would help me to do it. You have the advantage of being in a Christian school and studying hard with a curriculum based on Christian principles. You also have the advantage of reading your Bible daily, memorizing Scripture, and asking God to help you. God has a unique and special plan for each of your lives, so it is very important that you do your very best in school and learn as much as you can about God and His Word in order to be prepared for whatever God has in store for you. He wants to help you with everything—from your relationships to schoolwork, even that math or English that you don't think you will ever need! You are so special to Him and to me! One of my favorite Scriptures is Proverbs 3:5–6 (NKJV), which says, "Trust in the LORD with all your heart, and lean not on your own understanding; in all your ways acknowledge Him, and He shall direct your paths." If you allow God to control your lives, you will be amazed where He will take you! I have found that to be true for me! So how do you plan to glorify God with your lives?

CONNIVER

Grandkids, this is one of those stories that I was hesitant to write about, because I wasn't certain that it would hold your attention, or maybe that it would show how Grandpa's mind worked deviously. This story occurred when Grandpa was seven or eight years old in Bell, California. Grandpa had a friend who lived across the road from us and was one of the most explosive people he has ever known. This neighbor boy would lose his temper over the slightest provocation and just go ballistic. He would get violent and tear things up or try to hurt people. Great-Grandpa and Great-Grandma were probably not aware of his aggressiveness or they would have been hesitant about allowing me to play with this kid. Most of the young kids in the neighborhood were afraid of Danny, but I usually got along with him okay. Perhaps he was a little afraid of me, so he was less apt to lose his temper with me. However, there were a few times when he did totally lose his temper with me, and one of those times, he went berserk. I can't remember what I did to provoke him, but he went crazy. He picked up a small garden shovel and was trying to slash me with it. I did not have anything to protect myself from him, so I ran like a wild man, and Danny chased me, screaming and hollering. He chased me across the road, and I was just trying to get into my house. Grandkids, believe me, I was running like a scared rabbit. Danny wanted to hurt me, and I was very much aware of my predicament. I finally made it to the back steps, stumbled into the house, and locked the screen door. I thought I was finally safe, but Danny ran up the back steps and began to demolish the screen in the door. I can't remember for sure about this, but I think one of my sisters came to my rescue. She yelled at him, and he came back to reality and walked home. I am quite sure that one of my parents talked with Danny's parents and tried to make them aware of his violent tendencies.

I am sure it took a while for Grandpa to play with Danny again, but eventually it happened. I probably should not have been allowed to be alone with Danny without adult supervision, but there we were playing with each other again. I never again trusted Danny, but we usually had lots of fun together. He had two gigantic tortoises in his backyard, and we could actually ride on them. Grandpa's mind was always conniving, though. What would I do if Danny lost his evil, wicked temper again? Grandkids, you know exactly what happened. Once again I can't remember what I did to provoke him to lose his temper, but lose it he did. Danny did not grab a garden shovel this time, but he picked up some good-sized rocks and began to throw them at me vehemently. One more time I ran like a wild rabbit, but while running I looked up and saw the neighbor's large picture window. Our neighbor was an elderly woman who was not too friendly. I remember that she had a high cement block fence between our house and hers to keep us out of her yard. Instead of running to my house, I ran toward that large picture window. Danny was so angry that his rational mind was gone. He just wanted to hurt me. I ran to that window and stopped, and Danny thought he had me. He angrily threw one of his rocks at me, and I ducked. I heard a crash, and then Danny and I both realized what had happened. He just smashed Miss Crotchety's large picture window. He knew he was "dead meat," and now it was his turn to run like a scared rabbit. I walked to my house with a little smugness and pride. I had gotten my vengeance. Things became pretty crazy for a few hours. Now the neighbor lady went ballistic. She blamed me at first, and then, after some discussion with me and Great-Grandma, realized that Danny was the culprit. Danny got into some major trouble, and I got off scot-free. I really don't think my parents ever realized how much of a conniver their sweet, little, innocent son was.

Grandkids, be careful who you choose as friends. Someday you will probably be a parent. Please be aware who your children's friends are. Just because they are church kids does not automatically mean that they are appropriate. Just be careful. Someday I will be in Heaven and won't be here to warn you.

> "Never pay back evil for evil to anyone. Respect what is right in the sight of all men. If possible, so far as it depends on you, be at peace with all men. Never take your own revenge, beloved, but leave room for the wrath of God, for it is written, 'VENGEANCE IS MINE, I WILL REPAY,' says the Lord.
>
> ROMANS 12:17-21 (NASB)

HORNETS

Most people have had the experience of being stung by a hornet, wasp, yellow jacket, or honey bee. It seems that these wonderful creations of God become more aggressive in the fall. I remember getting stung by two wasps simultaneously on the back of my neck once in the early fall and had problems with my neck for three months. I actually went to the chiropractor several times, because my neck and shoulders became so stiff and painful.

Another time, Joey and I were playing basketball when he got stung by a yellow jacket. He began to react to the sting almost immediately. His skin was becoming blotchy and both of us were pretty concerned as his symptoms worsened. I called a nurse friend and asked her if I should take him to the hospital. Her response was "only if you want him to live." We jumped in the car and began driving to Reed City Hospital. I was driving sixty-five in a twenty-five-mile-an-hour zone. I drove down Main Street and came to U.S. 10. We turned left and sped out of Evart. I was driving very fast and passing cars when needed. Joey's skin became more flushed, and he was struggling to breathe. Grandpa was very scared and prayed as hard as he had ever prayed. I was driving over a hundred miles per hour as we approached the outskirts of Reed City. I then slowed down a little bit, turned left at the second intersection, and then was quickly at the Reed City Emergency Room. Joey continued to struggle to breathe as we walked into emergency. I think they gave him an injection with an Epi

Pen, plus other medications. He slowly but surely began to breathe easier, and his skin lost some of its blotchiness. After several hours we returned home very tired, but relieved. Grandpa and Grandma had no idea that Joey was allergic to bee stings but surely found out in a hurry that he was.

A different time, when Grandpa was in ninth grade, he took a stroll into the woods on a sunny Sunday afternoon. It was in early September and a rather warm day. I had walked quite a distance into the woods and passed through a fence. This was the first time I had ever been in those woods, and I was exploring for future squirrel hunting. I remember suddenly hearing a loud buzzing sound. My curiosity was aroused, and I kept moving closer to that loud buzz. I continued to move even closer, and the buzz got louder and louder. Grandkids, what I did not realize is that I had found a honey tree. I did locate the tree and watched as many, many honey bees were flying around it. Suddenly, I was surrounded by a swarm of bees. It seemed that there were millions of bees flying around my head with a tremendous buzz in my ears. It was like someone had thrown a blanket over my head. Studies say that people will react to a crisis by fighting, freezing, or going into flight. I did two of them. I was swatting bees vehemently and running like a wild man. When I came to the fence that I had earlier crawled through, I just hurdled it like an Olympic champion. Fear can give a person extraordinary strength, and I was terrified! I don't know how far I ran, but I finally realized that I was no longer being swarmed. When those bees surrounded me, I could feel them touching my face, arms, and hands. I stopped running and tried to get control of my emotions, and to get my heart to calm down. Then it struck me that I had not been stung even one time. I thought that I would have been stung many times. Was it God's protection or my guardian angel one more time rescuing me? Maybe honey bees are just much nicer than I realized. Over these many years I have wondered many, many times why those bees never stung me. Nevertheless, I walked back to the house very thankful for God's protection.

This next story is about hornets. I was push-mowing part of Great-Grandpa and Great-Grandma's yard. What Grandpa did not know is that there was a hive of underground hornets right where he was mowing. Those hornets are not large, but they surely do have a powerful sting. Grandpa just happened to mow directly over the entrance of the hornets' nest and then walk over it. One more time I was swarmed, mainly over my lower body. I literally had my legs covered in hornets, and that time I was getting stung. Yes, Grandkids, I went crazy again. I ran like a wild man and somehow stripped my clothing off as I ran. Thankfully I did leave my underwear on. Grandkids, brace yourselves, and let your imagination roll. I was running in my "whitey tighties" and did a swan dive into Betsy and Joey's small swimming pool. The giant splash must have scared the hornets off, because they were gone. I am very thankful I had a pair of baggy sweatpants on, because most of the hornets could not sting me, so I only got stung twenty-six times. Thank God that I am not allergic to bee stings!

"Give thanks in all circumstances; for this is the will of God in Christ Jesus for you."

1 THESSALONIANS 5:18 (ESV)

Grandkids, you may be asking how in the world Grandpa could give thanks after getting stung twenty-six times. It would have been much worse if I was wearing tighter pants. I would probably have been stung dozens of times. Always try to keep perspective even when bad things happen to you.